The Bush
Was

But Not
Consumed

Also by Eric H. F. Law
published by Chalice Press

The Wolf Shall Dwell with the Lamb

Inclusion

The Bush Was BLAZING But Not Consumed

Developing a Multicultural Community Through Dialogue and Liturgy

by Eric H. F. Law

Chalice  Press
St. Louis, Missouri

Biblical quotations, unless otherwise noted, are from the *New Revised Standard Version Bible*, copyright 1989, Division of Christian Education of the National Council of the Churches of Christ in the USA. Used by permission.

Cover design: Kris Vculek
Art Director: Michael Domínguez

Visit Chalice Press on the World Wide Web at
www.chalicepress.com

10 9 8 7 6 5 4 3   00 01

Law, Eric H. F.
    The bush was blazing but not consumed / Eric H. F. Law
        p.   cm.
    ISBN 0-8272-0222-9
    1. Christianity and culture—United States. 2. Multiculturalism—Religious aspects—Christianity. 3. Dialogue—Religious aspects—Christianity. 4. Reconciliation—Religious aspects—Christianity. 5. Liturgics. 6. Worship programs. 7. Burning bush. 8. Los Angeles (Calif.)—Church history—20th century. I. Title.
    BR526.L27 1996   96-34936
    261.8'34—dc20   CIP

Printed in the United States of America

Dedication:

In loving memory of my father,
Law Kwok-Nam,
whose irrepressible spirit
to improve and refine
whatever he was creating
permeates
my life and work.

Contents

Preface

As I was working on this book, I kept thinking how much richer it would be if my readers could immediately respond to what I was writing. It is paradoxical to write a book about the dialogue process as a way to develop a multicultural community without the element of dialogue with my readers. Yet, this is the limit of the book form as a mass medium—it is a one-way communication in which I have little opportunity to benefit from my readers' insights, nor do I have the chance to clarify, explain and expand on concepts that are not clear or insufficient. For this reason, I need to use these introductory pages to clarify some assumptions that I have taken for granted.

I have used terms and processes in this book previously described in my earlier book, *The Wolf Shall Dwell with the Lamb: A Spirituality for Leadership in a Multicultural Community* (St. Louis: Chalice Press, 1993). To gain a stronger background in understanding the material in this book, especially the last four chapters, I recommend that readers read my previous book, where I devoted a number of pages to explaining such concepts as power distance, power analysis, and group media, and processes such as Mutual Invitation, Photolanguage, and Community Bible Study. These concepts and processes are integral parts of the dialogue process.

This book is in some way a continuation of what I had started in *Wolf/Lamb*. It is an expansion of the last chapter, "Liturgy as Spiritual Discipline for Leadership in a Multicultural Community." The discipline of engaging in the dialogue process like a liturgy is a theme that runs through this volume.

In this book, I attempt to provide a theological justification for developing multicultural communities. However, this discussion about the positive aspects of developing a multicultural community does not negate the important work of monocultural communities. The words *multicultural community* often connote the image of a melting pot in which all the uniqueness of the different cultural groups will disappear so that they can become one. To many minority groups in North America, this image implies that all minority cultures are to lose their own identity and become like the historically dominant culture. The history of race relations in North America has precipitated the need for minority communities to separate themselves from the historically domi-nant culture in order to defend and regain their own identities. Thus, we must respect the need for all cultural groups to have their own monocultural environment in which they can do the work of building up their self-esteem and community identity.

A multicultural community as I describe it in this book is not a melting pot, but a dynamic process in which the various cultural groups maintain their identities while engaging them-selves in a constructive dialogue with each other. A true multicultural community seeks to maintain a balance of power, communication, and authenticity among the different cultural groups. No one group in this dynamic process will dominate, nor will any be made disadvantaged. One way to establish this balance is to support and respect the different groups' need for sharing within the comfort of their own cultural boundaries. For collective cultural groups, this intra-cultural dialogue is essential for them to establish their sense of power as a community. As they share their experience and insight arrived from the intra-cultural dialogue, the communication is stronger and clearer and the information is more authentic. This intra-cultural dialogue of a monocultural community is therefore an essential part of the overall process of furthering positive intercultural relations. In order to develop a constructive multicultural community, a leader must learn to discern when to respect the various cultural groups' need to be separate and when to invite them to come together for intercultural dialogue.

I also do not want to define multicultural community too narrowly. I use the word *community* to include not just long-term communities, such as multicultural congregations, but also short-time gatherings such as multicultural group meetings, liturgies, celebrations, and conferences. In other words, the work of devel-oping a multicultural community is an ongoing process that must be utilized at almost every gathering of people in our richly diverse society.

The term *dialogue*, as used in this book, is not simply a conversation between two persons. I use the term specifically to mean "an interchange of thoughts, feelings, and beliefs on a common subject between two or more persons of differing views." The primary purpose of dialogue is for each person to learn from the other so that he or she can change and grow. The "dialogue process" is the structure, sequence, and techniques used to facilitate a dialogue between persons or groups.

I also want to clarify how I have used the term *culture* in this book. I define culture as learned values, beliefs, perceptions, assumptions, patterns, and practices—both conscious and un-conscious—that enable us to perceive, interpret, evaluate, and respond to life and the world. Culture, as defined here, is not limited to race and ethnicity, even though for many of us, race and ethnicity constitute major parts of our cultural makeup. Other components that contribute to a person's culture can include gender, age, physical ability, sexual orientation, eco-nomic status, religion, marital status, education, community, work, family structure, and individual interests and experiences.

When I use the phrase *interracial dialogue*, I am specifically referring to a dialogue process that involves two or more groups of different racial and ethnic backgrounds. This kind of dialogue process sometimes, but not always, involves managing two or more languages. The phrase *intercultural dialogue* can be an interracial dialogue but it can also be a dialogue among persons who have one or more of the different cultural components listed above. For example, an intercultural dialogue can be an intergenerational, intergender, or interreligious dialogue. The ex-amples I have used in this book cover a wide range of intercul-tural dialogue experiences. Some explicitly deal with racial, eth-nic, and language groups. Some deal with differences in commu-nication styles, genders, generations, economic status, and even ideologies.

Sometimes we cannot separate these issues neatly, as many of the examples I have used demonstrate. Yet the dialogue process remains the same. For example, I was working with a committee of church leaders to plan a conference on intercultural relationships among clergy of different racial backgrounds. One of the committee members asked, "I want to learn how I can tell whether a conflict has to do with race or if it is just an issue of competence."

"In general," I replied, "when a person says there is racial discrimination going on here, we have to take it seriously. Whether it is 'racial' or not, it presents an issue that you must deal with. If you don't, it *will* become a racial issue. The only way to deal with it is to invite people to enter into a dialogue process. In the process, they will learn and respect each other's perspectives. The community that is developed through the dialogue process will determine what the issues are. The intercultural dialogue process does not just deal with racial issues; it also enables the community to address any issues created by all the components of cultural differences."

Just as I suggested to the person above, to trust the dialogue process to reveal the truth about different issues, I invite the readers to engage in a dialogue with this book. I do not expect my readers to agree with everything that I have presented in this book. I consider what I have done here as merely the beginning of a dialogue. Some readers will find the material inspiring, while others may disagree and even be offended by it. The point is not that we have to agree, but that we begin the dialogue. Whatever your reaction is, respect it and explore what caused it. Try out some of the dialogue techniques presented in this book. Engage in dialogue with others in your community. Let the dialogue begin.

Acknowledgments

I want to thank the United Methodist Church, especially the California-Pacific Conference and Bishop Roy Sano, for trusting and giving me numerous opportunities to test and refine many of the dialogue processes ever since I started my consulting ministry five years ago. I send my gratitude to Bishop Chester Talton, Suffragan Bishop of the Episcopal Diocese of Los Angeles, for his faithful support of the Intercultural Dialogue Programs after the 1992 Los Angeles riots. I am grateful to the following people whose thoughts and insights contributed to this book: Jose Carlo, Carmen Guerrero, Jerry Gifford, Nell Gibson, Ed Garren, Lucky Altman, and Jeanne Yeo-Ishikawa. I give thanks for the hospitality of Mark and Virginia MacDonald at whose home the final outline of this book came together. I also want to thank Kent Steinbrenner for his gift for details in the English language. I thank Steve Rutberg for his nurturing presence while I was working on this book. Finally, I thank all the groups and individuals I have worked with in the last three years. Without their participation and feedback in the dialogue process, this book would not have become a reality.

CHAPTER ONE

A Fire that Consumed: The 1992 Los Angeles Riots

O n Thursday, April 30, 1992, the day after the Simi Valley jury returned its verdicts on the four police officers in the Rodney King case, I was sitting in a café in West Hollywood eating an early dinner with a friend. Many voices were quarreling in my head—what to feel...what to think...what to do about the violent reactions to the not-guilty verdict? With my friend sitting across the table, I was looking forward to a constructive discussion. I thought another perspective might help.

The restaurant was full, but unusually quiet. A small television at the corner of the restaurant shot unappetizing images across the room. There was no escape from the media's obsession with fire, violence, and destruction. Between aerial shots of burning buildings, the television showed once again the scene from the previous day's coverage in which several African-American men pulled a white driver from his truck and beat him in the head and kicked him, knocking him to the ground. The commentators pronounced those words of disbelief again: "Where are the police? Where are the police?"

By now the majority of the patrons paid little attention to this scene, perhaps because they were already a little numbed by the repeated showing of this senseless act. But all the heads turned toward the television again when the commentator announced that a mini-mall was burning near Western and Crenshaw. Later, the patrons again paid attention to images of another burning building on Vermont near Wilshire. The riot was coming north.

1

When the television announced that the Beverly Center was bracing itself for the invading riot from the south and the east, the room took a moment to consider its significance. "Wait a minute, the Beverly Center is only about ten blocks from here. Is the riot going to hit West Hollywood?"

An instinctual voice in me said, "No way!" Immediately I was ashamed of this reaction. Did I feel this sense of security because West Hollywood was located right next to Beverly Hills? Did I really believe that the middle-upper-class walls that I had built around me were impenetrable from this kind of anger and rage? Then another voice vibrated through my body with a tremor of fear and it said, "Why not?" The walls could be falling.

My friend said, "Maybe we should stop at the market to stock up on food for the next few days just in case."

"Just in case of what?" I thought to myself. "Do we have so little faith in human nature? Do we assume that people cannot control their violent instincts once they are unleashed?"

After supper, we walked down Santa Monica Boulevard toward the market at an uncertain pace, still hoping that we could have more control over our lives than just buying food. I smelled the stench of plastic burning. I looked south and saw black smoke looming in the sky. As I read the writing in the sky—a message of rage and mistrust built up from centuries of injustice—I was screaming silently. But instead of calling for the police like the announcers had done, I was screaming silently for God: "Where is God? Where is God in this fire?" If I could not see God in this fire, then there was no redemption, no hope, no resurrection. An unholy fire was burning in Los Angeles. It was blazing hot, out of control. It blazed for four days and it consumed properties, lives—and, more tragically, our spirit and faith.

> For they are kindled like an oven, their heart burns within them; all night their anger smolders; in the morning it blazes like a flaming fire. All of them are hot as an oven, and they devour their rulers. All their kings have fallen; none of them calls upon me. Ephraim mixes himself with the peoples; Ephraim is a cake not turned. Foreigners devour his strength, but he does not know it; gray hairs are sprinkled upon him, but he does not know it. Israel's pride testifies against him; yet they do not return to the LORD their God, or seek him, for all this.
>
> Hosea 7:6–10

Fire is a symbol of destruction because of its power to consume. Independent of whether the people's anger and rage were justified, the Los Angeles riots of 1992 were fires that consumed not only physical things. These riots, along with many other previous riots in this and other cities, were symbolic fires that had been kindled in the oven of a long history of injustice in the United States. This fire burned within the people who believed that even with solid proof like a videotape of the actual beating of Rodney King, there was still no justice. Their anger blazed like a flaming fire, consuming their sense of morality, justice, civility, and humanity. As they acted out their rage against the injustice, they could not see that their action was no better then those who instigated the injustice in the first place.

They also defiled the law. They rebelled and devoured the "rulers" and "kings" of the land by giving no regard to its sense of order because they could not trust the laws and the rulers anymore. When they became part of the blazing and consuming fire, they did not know that their strength to do true justice was diminishing. Foreign forces of evil—those twin principalities and powers called racism and classism—were winning one more time, perpetuating the stereotypical image of African Americans as people prone to violence and a disregard for the law.

As they became the flame that blazed with justification, they themselves were consumed. "Gray hairs are sprinkled upon" their youthful energy to hold on to righteousness and faithfulness in the face of adversity. Somewhere in the back of their minds, their humanity testified to them that this was wrong, but they could not help it. Somewhere hidden inside their hearts, they knew that they needed to seek God—the God of reconciliation, the God of righteousness and truth, the God of peace and true justice, the God of creation—but they could not find the energy or strength to do that because they were the fire that blazed, and in the end they consumed themselves.

CHAPTER TWO

The Bush Was Blazing, But Not Consumed: In Search of God in the Fire

One year after the 1992 Los Angeles riots, I was the play-wright-in-residence of an interdisciplinary theater project funded by a FEMA grant. The purpose of the project was to educate young people in the greater Los Angeles area in under-standing a disaster like the 1992 riots. My role, in collaboration with other actors, artists, and activists, was to help a group of high school students create a short play based on their research of past riots in Los Angeles. We studied five different riots.

1. The Anti-Chinese Riot of 1871: A large group of white residents stormed into Chinatown on October 24, murdered 18 people, and set many buildings on fire. Only ten rioters were brought to trial. Eight were pronounced guilty and were sentenced from two to six years in prison. A year later, the California Supreme Court reversed the Los Angeles jury's verdict, saying, "Admitting that the defendants did all these things, still it does not follow by necessary legal conclusion that, after all, any person was actually murdered."

2. The Zoot Suit Riot of 1943: On June 7, a mob of more than one thousand soldiers, sailors and civilians broke into movie theaters, streetcars, and homes dragging out Mexicans and blacks—and, in particular, youths wearing "zoot-suits"—onto the street and stripped and beat them, while the police stood by or on occasion arrested the victims.

3. The Watts Riots of August 1965: Black residents of Watts and surrounding areas burned, looted, and battled with police for six days. Forty million dollars' worth of property was destroyed, 600 buildings were damaged or demolished, and more than 3,400 adults and 500 juveniles were arrested; 1,032 persons were injured, and 34 were killed. Twenty-six of the deaths were judged to be justifiable homicide, 16 were caused by officers of the Los Angeles Police Department, and 7 by the National Guard.

4. The police riot against the Chicano Moratorium in August 1970: The Chicano Moratorium began as a peaceful protest at Laguna Park against the Vietnam War. Without any provocation, 1,200 police officers invaded the gathering and occupied the park. Two Chicanos were killed and there were mass arrests. Later, police surrounded and attacked the bar and Rubén Salazar, a reporter for the *Los Angeles Times* and KMEX-TV, was killed. During the inquest, all seven jurors reached the rapid conclusion that the killing was unintended.

5. The 1992 riots: Triggered by the not-guilty verdict of the four policemen charged with the beating of Rodney King, starting from South Central Los Angeles, and spreading across the greater Los Angeles area, residents burned, looted, and battled with each other and with the police for three days. The anger and rage were reminiscent of the Watts riots in 1965.

After we did our initial research, an African-American student said, "I thought only black people and minorities rioted; I didn't know white people, police and soldiers also did it."

The response that came from the rest of the class was: "Oh yes, we are all capable of rioting," but perhaps for different reasons.

"What a relief!" She continued, "I thought there was something wrong with us black people." Since the 1992 and the Watts riots were covered heavily by the media all across the country, they became the defining events for what a riot should be. However, as we studied these events more closely, we began to see two different kinds of riots. The Anti-Chinese Riot, the Zoot Suit Riot, and the police riot against the Chicano Moratorium involved the majority's acting against a minority group because the majority perceived that a particular minority was a threat simply because they were different. The Watts riots and the 1992 riots involved a minority group's rebellion against an oppressive system controlled by the majority. In both cases there was much fear, violence, pain, loss, death, and destruction. As a playwright, I was trying to find the unifying theme for the dramatic piece we were creating. I could not help but feel that I was dealing with something very old—something that had been going on for a long time. I sensed that I was dealing with something that is almost part of nature, which resulted in the play's title, *The Nature of Riots*.

For the majority group, perhaps there was something in our human nature that made us feel insecure about ourselves, even though we were in control in every way. Perhaps as a reflex reaction to our insecurity, we became fearful and suspicious of those who were different. Perhaps in our striving for security and certainty, our very instinct to survive was driving us to disregard human civility and the rights of others. Do we dare to admit that our fragile egos were made to feel stronger when we put down others who were different? Even though large-scale riots with physical destruction that were perpetrated by the majority were not observable in the recent past, there is a kind of quiet riot going on in our society, in which the majority controls and manipulates the political, social, and economic system to continuously and quietly keep the minority groups at a disadvantage. The police officers' brutal beating of Rodney King and the jury's not-guilty verdict were just the occasional revelation of this quiet riot.

For the minority groups who are on the other side, enduring oppression created by the majority's insecurity, our impulse to stand up for ourselves and for our rage elevated by the long history of injustice may have driven us to rebel and dismiss the law of the land. Do we dare to admit that participation in anarchy can supply us with a dose of power and freedom for which we thirst? While the dust was settling from the indulgence of the minority groups' egos, the fear and insecurity of the majority were then reinforced. With their fear confirmed, the majority continued its quiet riot by creating an even more hostile environment—one that was drier and more flammable, and infested with more control, stereotypes, and prejudices. The two kinds of riots are related; they form a vicious cycle of control on one side of the wheel and rebellion on the other. These two sides keep the wheel of destruction turning: The minority's rebellion creates more fear for the majority, which in turn exercises more control, which then sets the stage for the next rebellion. This wheel of destruction has formed the source of the undercurrent that has moved and shaken the history of interracial relations in North America.

As the students explored the characters in the riots of Los Angeles past, they began to see that the riots depicted in the play were only the sporadic outbursts of this interracial undercurrent in the United States. Our long history of imposing a system of disadvantage onto minorities has made interracial relations in the United States barren, like a desert full of dry bushes ready to be ignited at any time and at any place. Interracial issues and intercultural conflicts are so "hot" that we tiptoe around them when we can. We pretend the issue does not exist until it gets so hot that we cannot ignore it any more. Then it flares up—burning out of control—and in so doing, confirms our greatest fear. Even when people with good intentions come together to develop an intercultural community, they are often surprised by how the fire just flares up out of control. The igniting spark could be a word, a look or an unconscious expression of an attitude. In our group of students, arguments would begin and accusations and judgments would fly across the room. Often, if these differences were not addressed constructively, people would leave with an overwhelming frustration that perhaps these attempts to create interracial harmony and intercultural community were hopeless and a waste of time and energy.

As I walk through the desert of interracial relations, where a fire can flare up and blaze as readily as a dry bush lit by a match, I must ask again: Where is the image of hope? Where is the good news? Where is God in the fire? As I searched for God in the fire, I rediscovered a fire image that is quite "unnatural"—the burning bush.

> Moses was keeping the flock of his father-in-law Jethro, the priest of Midian; he led his flock beyond the wilderness, and came to Horeb, the mountain of God. There the angel of the Lord appeared to him in a flame of fire out of a bush; he looked, and the bush was blazing, yet it was not consumed. Then Moses said, "I must turn aside and look at this great sight, and see why the bush is not burned up." When the Lord saw that he had turned aside to see, God called to him out of the bush, "Moses, Moses!" And he said, "Here I am." Then he said, "Come no closer! Remove the sandals from your feet, for the place on which you are standing is holy ground." He said further, "I am the God of your father, the God of Abraham, the God of Isaac, and the God of Jacob." And Moses hid his face, for he was afraid to look at God.
>
> Exodus 3:1–6

I was fascinated by the phrase "the bush was blazing, yet it was not consumed." How could that be? Fire, by nature, consumes. Most material that has been burned has been rendered useless. Wood turns into ashes. Metal objects melt in the intense heat, losing their intended useful shapes. We have learned to fear the destructiveness of fire just by viewing on television the buildings and forests burned and consumed by it. We were taught when we were very young not to play with fire, because it is dangerous. Fire also represents intense feeling—anger, rage, desire, etc. The fire of anger, for example, is often put down as something that hurts others and should be controlled. Fire, both physical and as a symbol of our intense emotions, is something we have learned to avoid or control because it does have the potential to consume us as well as others. The miraculous event of the calling of Moses was that "the bush was blazing, yet it was not consumed." In observing this "unnatural" phenomenon, Moses recognized the presence of God who commanded him to remove his sandals because he was standing on holy ground.

The burning bush, aside from being a symbol of the calling of Moses, becomes the image of hope in the brittle state of interracial relations in this country. God takes a symbol of fear, rage, and destruction and turns it into an empowering symbol that moves Moses into action—to liberate the children of Israel from slavery. Instead of being held hostage by fear and destruction, we too are called by God to embrace the fire as a source of energy that is creative and liberating. The burning bush is the hopeful image I was looking for. The hope is that we can somehow sanctify the interracial fire so that it will not consume, but rather reveal the existence and glory of God.

As I explored this hopeful symbol of a fire that does not consume, I came across another passage in scripture that spoke to this in more direct, powerful images. This passage from Daniel describes the story of Shadrach, Meshach, and Abednego, who were Jews appointed to oversee the affairs of the province of Babylon. They were accused of not paying heed to the king by worshiping the golden image made by King Nebuchadnezzar. The king summoned the three and commanded them to worship the golden statue with the threat that if they did not, they would be thrown into a furnace of blazing fire. But they refused.

> Then Nebuchadnezzar was so filled with rage against Shadrach, Meshach, and Abednego that his face was distorted. He ordered the furnace heated up seven times more than was customary, and ordered some of the strongest

guards in his army to bind Shadrach, Meshach, and Abednego and to throw them into the furnace of blazing fire....Because the king's command was urgent and the furnace was so overheated, the raging flames killed the men who lifted Shadrach, Meshach, and Abednego. But the three men, Shadrach, Meshach, and Abednego fell down, bound, into the furnace of blazing fire. Then King Nebuchadnezzar was astonished and rose up quickly. He said to his counselors, "Was it not three men that we threw bound into the fire?" They answered the king, "True, O king." He replied, "But I see four men unbound, walking in the middle of the fire, and they are not hurt; and the fourth has the appearance of a god."

Daniel 3:19–25

Nebuchadnezzar then ordered the three to come out of the furnace. When the king discovered the fire did not harm a hair of the three, he glorified the God of Shadrach, Meshach, and Abednego and promoted them. Acting contrary to what most people would do in order to survive, Shadrach, Meshach, and Abednego entered the fire knowing that God would protect them. Not only were they not consumed by the fire, the presence of God was recognized in their action—the fourth person in the fire who "has the appearance of a god."

The sanctification of the fire is the recognition of God in the fire. In affirming the presence of God in the fire, we can stop being afraid of the fire. Instead, we can enter the fire knowing that God will protect and lead us through this ordeal with the forces of liberation, justice, and peace. In our "unnatural" act against our instinct to survive, God is the one who is glorified; the mighty work of God is seen and heard and understood.

As the globalization of our economy continues and inter- and intra-continental migration persists, we will be sure to experience an increased frequency of conflicts based on differences in race, gender, and generations. We can no longer assume that community will form "naturally" around us as we live and work in our society today. Communities that are formed based on common interests and backgrounds are effortless to create. In fact, they just happen naturally, because like-minded people gravitate to each other. However, with increased diversity of the population and the mobility of people in this country, the "natural" communities are increasingly harder to either find or form, resulting in many individuals feeling isolated and alone. At the same time, our instinct to survive pulls us farther apart with suspicion and defensiveness, making it even harder to form any kind of multicultural community. This may be the cause of many churches' decline in membership in the last ten years.

In the attempt to create a multicultural community, many churches simply put people of diverse cultural backgrounds under one roof and expect them to get along with each other without facilitating any constructive dialogue. As a result, the different groups' natural instincts take over and the interracial fire starts burning. As long as we are human beings with our insecurity, our instinct to survive, and our rebellious rage, interracial conflicts will blaze out of control in these attempts to create intercultural communities. The unholy fire will burn if no effort is made to sanctify the fire by recognizing and affirming the presence of God. If our churches are going to grow into a multicultural community, we can no longer rely on our natural instinct to form a community. Instead, we must act intentionally—sometimes against our instinct—in order to develop a community in which people of different backgrounds can not only tolerate each other but are able to understand and appreciate each other even though they may not agree. We cannot rely on our natural instinct, but must focus on God through Jesus Christ, who will give us the courage to walk into the fire—to die to our old selfish instinct and be resurrected in the new life where we struggle to build and tend the holy fire that will burn but not consume. We must invite God to transform the unholy fire into the fire of Pentecost.

What does this holy fire look and feel like? Perhaps by exploring the positive aspects of fire, we can gain some more insight into the practical aspect of building and tending a holy fire. Fire gives off heat and provides warmth when it is cold. But a useful fire has to be contained and attended to, or it will blaze out of control and consume more than we intend. We burn wood in our fireplace to keep the house warm in the winter, but starting a fire elsewhere in the house would be quite dangerous. The other place where we permit fire is in the kitchen. Fire, when tempered, cooks our food just right for our nourishment. But if we don't pay attention to our cooking, the fire will burn our food, rendering it inedible. Fire is also used in a kiln to create useful tools and utensils that can enhance our lives. Fire also can be used in a refining process to purify substances. Whenever a fire is created for useful purposes, we must give great care in maintaining and containing the fire.

For many years, I volunteered my time every summer as a chaplain for a summer camp. Every evening, I would search for a group that had decided to start a campfire. I was attracted to a campfire because I knew the children would finally calm down and develop a sense of community surrounding a campfire. As they arrived at the site of the campfire, the children were still not quite together as a group. Some complained about the long hike. Some complained about having to carry the food for everybody. The camp counselor was inevitably dealing with minor injuries— a scraped knee here or a cut finger there. Some experienced campers were off searching for kindling or dry wood to start the fire. Chaos took hold of the situation for a moment. Then those who went searching for firewood returned. With some disagreement on what was the best technique to start a fire, they finally got it going. Suddenly a new spirit emerged from the fire. The heat, the light, the sparks, and the sound of the fire got everyone's attention. The children, without any herding, converged to the fire. They stared at the fire as the sun set. As they cooked the food, they continued to focus on the fire. Was the food getting enough heat? Was the food getting burned? Was the food ready? They threw in more wood when the fire was diminishing. They backed off from the heat when the fire was too strong. They were aware of where the fire was at all times because they knew that if they did not, the fire might get out of hand.

After dinner, another kind of liturgy began—making "S'mores." The campers carefully put sticks through marshmallows, helping each other—especially the younger ones, who had less experience in toasting the perfect marshmallow. Again, they watched the fire carefully as it toasted the white cottony balls on the tips of their sticks. Some preferred the marshmallow to be flaming, and then blew the fire out quickly. Some preferred the marshmallow to be toasted gently and slowly by the invisible heat. When the first few marshmallows were ready, there was always a demonstration of how S'mores were properly made; this for the benefit of any young children who had not yet experienced the delightful combination of marshmallows, chocolate bars, and graham crackers. After everyone had consumed their S'mores, they stared at the fire some more, mesmerized by its brightness, danger, warmth, and power. Pretty soon someone would start singing a song. Everyone would join in. It did not matter what the song was, as long as everyone sang it. Song after song, the fire kept it going. Occasionally, someone would tell a story. With the fire and the shadows, everyone listened attentively, following every word, image, and mood of the storyteller. They could stay up all night doing this—all because they were sitting around a campfire.

Have you ever tried to get a group of kids to sing campfire songs without a fire? Have you tried to coerce a group of kids to eat charred, burned food without a campfire? With a fire and the "liturgies" around it, children seem more willing to take risks and do things that they normally don't. The fire's presence allows them to be less inhibited. The campfire is a fire that does not consume, but rather nurtures and builds the community. When the fire is attended to with great care, we can help people to focus on activities that build a sense of community, and also listen to each other attentively. The parable of the campfire gives us a glimpse of the hopeful sign of the holy fire, the burning bush.

When we develop a multicultural community, we must gather around the burning bush like we gather around a campfire. The burning bush draws people of different backgrounds together and gives them warmth and nourishment in the dark, cold night of the interracial desert. The burning bush demands respect from the people—"take off your sandals"—for God and for each other. The burning bush necessitates cooperation in tending the fire so that it will not flare out and consume. The burning bush encourages people to take risks and do the unnatural by dealing with hot topics such as stereotypes, prejudice, discrimination, racism, and interracial conflict, with an honest sharing of personal stories and receptive, attentive listening. The burning bush forms a multicultural community with a liturgy of hopeful songs and redemptive, reconciling stories. The burning bush holds the multicultural community together by maintaining a constructive tension between the danger of risk-taking on the one side and the joy of reconciliation and forgiveness on the other. The burning bush empowers the multicultural community to go out into the world and foster interracial harmony by using its heat to fashion dialogue tools that we can demonstrate and use. The burning bush raises up our multicultural community to be a light on the hill showing the world that there is a constructive approach to interracial conflicts.

Let your light shine before others, so that they may see your good works and give glory to your Father in heaven.
Matthew 5:16

CHAPTER THREE

Fire as Divine Judgment and Purification

While we hold up the image of the burning bush as our vision of a multicultural community, we must not forget that the image of fire has other significant roles in our search for God in the fire. As a faithful reader of scripture, I must not simply use whatever images and ideas support my cause and disregard the other ideas and images I do not find helpful. Therefore, to continue my search for God in the fire, I must continue to explore other references to fire in both the Hebrew and Christian scriptures.

The image of fire predominantly signified the presence of God in the Hebrew Scriptures. God appeared to Abraham to set forth the covenant with him in the form of a fire (Genesis 15:17). God called Moses to be the agent of delivery for the Israelites in the form of the burning bush (Exodus 3:2; Acts 7:30). God led Israel out of Egypt in the pillar of fire by night in the wilderness (Exodus 13:21–22; 14:24; Numbers 9:15–16; 14:14; Deuteronomy 1:33; Nehemiah 9:12, 19; Psalms 78:124; 105:39; Isaiah 4:5). On Mount Sinai, God again appeared as fire to Moses and the Israelites (Exodus 119:18; 24:178; Deuteronomy 4:11–36; 5:4–26; 9:10, 15; 18:16; 1 Kings 18:24; Hebrews 12:18). In the Christian Scriptures, in the vision of John (Revelation 1:14; 2:18) Christ appeared with "eyes of fire," and "tongues of fire" accompanied the Holy Spirit as it descended(Acts 2).

I was, however, very perplexed by scripture's depictions of God's appearance through fire as divine judgment and purification of sin where consumption by fire was interpreted as the punishment of the wicked and the unrighteous. Destruction by fire was perceived to be the wrath of God (Psalm 89:46b—89:47; Jeremiah 4:4; 15:14; 21:12; Lamentations 1:13; 2:3; Ezekiel 22:31) or the jealousy of God (Deuteronomy 4:24; Psalm 69:5; Ezekiel 38:22; 39:6; Zephaniah 1:18). Likewise, the Christian Scriptures also cited fire as an element of judgment (Matthew 3:10, 12; 5:22; 13:40; 18:8–9; 25:41; Mark 9:43–48; Luke 17:29; 2 Peter 3:7; Jude 23; Revelation 8:7; 9:18; 11:5; 14:10; 19:20; 20:9–15; 21:8).[1]

In my theology of a benevolent God who was good and creative, I found myself struggling again to make sense of the fire in the 1992 riots in Los Angeles. My theology allowed me to interpret the destructive fire as human fallen-ness—as human beings' inability to be faithful to God's commandments to love one another and take care of creation. But I was not ready to entertain the idea that God was in the fire to punish us. I thought I was protecting God's reputation; but truthfully, I was really protecting my theology, which at this time was limiting who God really was. If I were to be a faithful reader of Scripture, I had to recognize that the evidence of a jealous and angry God was too strong and prevalent to be ignored. With much resistance and fear, I decided to come out of my comfortable theological closet and enter into a world of uncertainty, hoping for exciting new discoveries. When I was finally open to the possibility that God could be angry and jealous, I was free to ask: Why would God be jealous and angry? How does fire as divine judgment reconcile with fire as the presence of God? How does recognition of God's presence in the fire connect with fire as a purification of sin? I believe the answer lies in further exploring the image of fire as the presence of God.

A fire is holy when we recognize the presence of God in it. "Were not our hearts burning within us while he was talking to us on the road, while he [Jesus] was opening the scriptures to us?" (Luke 24:32) A holy fire is a fire of understanding. It helps us see our mission more clearly. It helps us hear God's call more accurately. We are empowered to act according to God's commands. We act creatively rather than destructively when we encounter injustice around us. When we see the healing power of God at

---

[1] The biblical references of the meaning and symbol of fire are taken from *The Interpreter's Dictionary of the Bible* (Nashville: Abingdon Press, 1962), Volume 2, pp. 268–269.

work, we no longer are ablaze with our anger and rage, and out of control; instead we can become a gentle light on the hill where all can see the glory of God.

A fire becomes destructive if we use the fire for our own gain and do not respect the presence of God in it. Instead of focusing on God's power to heal and reverse injustice, we take justice into our own hands, and allow our win/lose human sense of justice to take over—an eye for an eye. When we become the judge ourselves, we forget that God is the only judge. Without God, our rage blazes out of control and we become the fire ourselves, consuming everything around us and consuming ourselves. When we become the fire, we are displacing God from the fire. The fire ceases to be holy because we are playing God. Ultimately it is adultery about which God is most angry and jealous. This is what divine judgment by fire is about: When we become the fire, we are consumed by the fire.

Divine judgment does not have the same connotation of "judgment" as we use the word secularly. We tend to think of judgment as judging based on our own conscious and unconscious values. The end product of judging is the determination of who is right or wrong, good or bad. Divine judgment by fire is not about finding out who is right or wrong among us; it is about finally learning that God is the one who makes the final judgment, not us. "There is one lawgiver and judge who is able to save and to destroy. So who, then, are you to judge your neighbor?" (James 4:12) Divine judgment is about being forced to see that we are not God and cannot judge each other as if we are God. Only God is God. In a sense, divine judgment by fire is the final recognition of the presence of God in the fire.

> For throughout all their journeys the cloud of the Lord was upon the tabernacle by day, and fire was in it by night, in the sight of all the house of Israel.
>
> Exodus 40:38, NJB

While the Israelites were wandering in the wilderness, the center of the community was the tabernacle, where God's presence was recognized and revered. The image is that of a refinery—the fire that purifies the raw material and the cloud of smoke that the fire produces through the chimney. Israel's wandering in the wilderness can then be interpreted as a refining process in which the Israelites were judged again and again for their adultery in seeking after false gods. Each time the divine judgment was issued, their relationship with God was refined and purified, and their covenant with God was renewed.

Divine judgment in the Christian context is not the end, but the beginning, because, as Christians, we believe in redemption through Jesus Christ. Like the Israelites in the wilderness, when we are confronted with divine judgment, we can repent of our sin in seeking after false gods. In our confession, we see ourselves more honestly as the created, while we see God more clearly as the creator. In responding to divine judgment, we gain a clearer understanding of our covenant with God. As human beings, we will find ourselves falling into sin again. But divine judgment will confront us each time, making our vision of God and of our ministries purer and stronger. Therefore, the purification of our vision of God is not a one-time deal. It is through repeated experiences of divine judgment that we continue to see more and more clearly our relationship with God. It is a lifelong process, and it is a process that will continue from generation to generation.

In the multicultural society we live in, the temptation to "play God" by judging, controlling, and disregarding others' human rights is so much greater when we allow our human survival instinct to take over. In every turn of events that causes us to become insecure and uncertain of our future, we face the danger of losing sight of God. How can we maintain our openness to divine judgment and allow God to purify us each time we fall into the sin of fearing, judging, controlling, and putting down others who are different?

> For I received from the Lord what I also handed on to you, that the Lord Jesus on the night when he was betrayed took a loaf of bread, and when he had given thanks, he broke it and said, "This is my body that is for you. Do this in remembrance of me." In the same way he took the cup also, after supper, saying, "This cup is the new covenant in my blood. Do this, as often as you drink it, in remembrance of me." For as often as you eat this bread and drink the cup, you proclaim the Lord's death until he comes.
>
> 1 Corinthians 11:23–26

Christian communities move through the same eucharistic liturgy over and over again. Each time we reenact this liturgy, we renew our covenant with God through Jesus Christ. In this refining process, we recognize our humanness and God's divine presence, and we see God more clearly, resulting in more accurate discernment of our ministry. In order to develop multicultural community, we can apply the same principle of liturgy to help us purify our vision of God and our ministry as a reconciling people. In our liturgies of dialogue and reconciliation, we continue, as people of diverse backgrounds, to purify our covenant with God. In our liturgies, we invite God to be in the center of the interracial fire when we see and feel a fire burning inside us. In our liturgies, we sanctify the fire by withholding our judgment of each other, but allow God's reconciling power to be the only judge. In our liturgies, we learn to listen to each other openly and speak to each other honestly, while we appeal to God to help us discern the next step.

Divine judgment by fire and recognizing God's presence in the fire are different sides of the same concept. Purification of sin through fire is the process of allowing divine judgment to confront us again and again, helping us to recognize God's presence more clearly each time. The fire of purification reaffirms and renews our covenant with God. This fire of purification is the burning bush that keeps a multicultural community alive and together. The burning bush judges and redeems us when we sin against God and each other. The burning bush purifies the vision of the multicultural community, shaping and reshaping it, never allowing it to become stagnant and adulterous. When we gather around the burning bush, we will be warmed by the fire in the cold, dark night of fear and avoidance. When we gather around the burning bush, we will be protected by the smoke cloud that it produces when the bright ray of destruction is beating down on us. As we gather around the burning bush, God's presence is recognized and affirmed and we are not afraid to walk into the fire of interracial dialogue and reconciliation. As we gather around the burning bush, we are cleansed, renewed, and energized to continue our work of justice and peace in this barren land of social injustice and rage.

In this book, I will attempt to describe this multicultural community that gathers around the burning bush and how we can practically and faithfully develop such a community. In chapters 4 through 7, I will examine the barriers that block us from moving toward a true multicultural community. These barriers are our obsession over the unholy fire, our preoccupation with the golden calf, and our building of the Tower of Babel. Chapters 8 through 13 examine the theoretical and practical aspects of how to develop a true multicultural community. We will focus on how to design and facilitate intercultural dialogue processes and liturgies as the principal tools for developing a multicultural community.

CHAPTER FOUR

Obsession over the Unholy Fire

Then they seized [Jesus] and led him away, bringing him into the high priest's house. But Peter was following at a distance. When they had kindled a fire in the middle of the courtyard and sat down together, Peter sat among them. Then a servant-girl, seeing him in the firelight, stared at him and said, "This man also was with him." But he denied it, saying, "Woman, I do not know him." A little later someone else, on seeing him, said, "You also are one of them." But Peter said, "Man, I am not." Then about an hour later still another kept insisting, "Surely this man also was with him; for he is a Galilean." But Peter said, "Man, I do not know what you are talking about!" At that moment, while he was still speaking, the cock crowed. The Lord turned and looked at Peter. Then Peter remembered the word of the Lord, how he had said to him, "Before the cock crows today, you will deny me three times." And he went out and wept bitterly.

Luke 22:54–62

The image of a group of people gathering around a fire usually connotes warmth and fellowship like that of a campfire. It might have involved sharing of thoughts, feelings, ideas, songs, and food. But it was not so with this fire around which Peter sat. This fire was not used as a positive force to draw people together for fellowship and mutual understanding. Instead, this fire was used as a searchlight of accusation. This was not a burning bush, but an unholy fire that consumes others with human judgment. Around this unholy fire, three people confronted Peter with the accusation that he was part of Jesus' group. But Peter avoided the confrontation by denying that he knew Jesus. Why? Perhaps he was afraid for his own safety. If Peter admitted that he was an associate of Jesus, the unholy fire might flare up and Peter might be handed over to the Romans to share the same fate as Jesus. His instinct to survive took over at that moment of accusation. He could not find himself admitting to being a follower of someone who was considered a loser. Fear is often generated by the mentality that there is a winning and a losing side—a right and a wrong. Fear was the coal of this unholy fire. This unholy fire left a scorching mark of guilt and sorrow on Peter when he realized what he had done.

Two days after the start of the Los Angeles riots, I had to go to New York City for a family gathering. I was relieved that I did not have to be in Los Angeles while the fire was still raging. As soon as I told people in New York that I was from Los Angeles, they all said how lucky I was to be away from the blazing city. I felt like Peter—sitting around an unholy fire listening to my friends and relatives taking sides. Some judged the African Americans for their misconduct, while my liberal friends insisted that I refer to the event with a neutral term by calling it an "uprising." Upon discovering that I was a consultant in intercultural concerns, some of my friends said, "That means business is going to be very good for you." In their win/lose mind-set, somebody had to be winning something in this event; it might as well be me. I just wanted to avoid the discussion. I denied the presence of God in the fire. I smiled and went along with whatever they were saying. I heard people asking me, "Aren't you from Los Angeles? What do you think? Where do you stand?" I was feeling very guilty that I was not remaining closer to the fire. Should I have canceled my trip to New York and remained in Los Angeles to do more constructive things such as starting a dialogue group? Should I have stayed in Los Angeles and worked with my bishop to develop a program that would help people deal with this fire?

The bottom line was that, like Peter, I was afraid. I actually imagined returning to Los Angeles to find my home burned down to the ground. Meanwhile, I was watching the New York TV coverage of the riot. Now they were showing new sensational images—Korean merchants holding rifles to protect their stores from the looters who, by the way, were not just African Americans. These images were shown in conjunction with an inflammatory report of an old incident involving a female Korean shopowner's shooting an African-American girl in South Central Los Angeles. Why were they bringing that up? Was it really that simple? Were we supposed to believe that the African Americans looted the Korean stores and the Korean Americans protected their property with guns simply because these two ethnic groups did not get along in the past? Something was not right as I fenced off mentally the words and images that those in the media were trying to impose on me. The riot was instigated by an unfair trial of a group of white police officers brutally beating up an African-American man. What does a group of people rebelling against the system have to do with two ethnic groups not getting along? The transition was incomprehensible to me.

What was wrong was that the riot was now being presented as a spectators' sport. It was not reported as a group of people rebelling against the system but a fight among the various ethnic minorities. I, the spectator, was led into the interracial arena to watch who was going to win and who was going to lose. I was prompted to choose a side. I was supposed to cheer my side on, and put down and judge the other side. The system was now off the hook. The principalities and powers called racism and classism continued to reign, once again reinforcing the stereotype that minority groups could not handle affairs on their own and there-fore required the majority to "take care" of them. That was when the massive police force and National Guard came into the camera's view. The system was the referee who would keep this fight among the minorities in control.

Months later, I was watching a local television newscast one evening. The sportscaster had a commentary on winning and losing. He said, "Winning is everything. When you win, you win! When you lose...." He paused deliberately and then screamed, "YOU ARE NOTHING!" He said this as if this was common knowledge.

His comment reminded me of an incident that I had long forgotten until now. When I was a freshman in college, I enjoyed playing squash because the game was played in an enclosed room. Unlike tennis, I did not have to spend so much energy chasing after the ball and could concentrate on hitting it. I also enjoyed playing the game alone and did not play with a partner frequently. One day as I was practicing, another student asked if I would like to play a game with him. I said, "Why not?"

As we played, I was losing, but I was having a very good time. So occasionally I would laugh, even though I was losing. He suddenly stopped and interrogated me, asking, "Why are you laughing? Don't you know you are losing?"

I was surprised by his remarks. The only words I could utter were, "It's because I am having a good time."

He looked at me in disbelief and left the court. Incidents like this one clearly demonstrate the problem some people have of needing to see things in a win/lose dichotomy. My squash partner seemed to have no reason to play unless there would be a winner and a loser. Furthermore, the pleasure of winning lies in seeing the other player or team losing. Without the loser, there is no winner. The winner depends on the loser in order to gain an identity. In other words, in order to maintain one's self-worth in a society that advocates this win/lose mentality, one needs only to look externally to find a loser, therefore, making oneself the winner. In such a society, one may overlook the possibility of developing an internal self-identity based on an independent exploration of self-worth and self-esteem.

With such a mind-set, who would want to lose in the United States? Losing means forfeiting one's identity. This abhorrence toward losing fuels the unholy fire. The Los Angeles riots were instigated by such a mentality. Surely with solid evidence such as the videotape, we had to win. But our justice system said the policemen won. When we were supposed to win and we did not, the anger flared and the fire burned. Many, in fact, believed that since they could not win in the legal system, they would win by destruction. One can almost hear them say, "When they saw that we were angry enough to destroy this city, they would listen." In fact, this destructive fire worked in influencing the outcome of the second trial, resulting in the conviction of the policemen. A sigh of relief spread across southern California: There won't be another riot! The unholy fire may have been avoided for the moment, but it did not go out. It became a glowing ember, ready to be ignited when the next wind of conflict blows.

This glowing ember has had a dampening effect on our ability to address interracial issues in the United States. Every time a public event was perceived as a potential interracial conflict, the police department talked about beefing up the force in case of civil unrest. The public was pitched into the win/lose mentality: Who is going to win this time? Then we were reminded that if the minority side lost, especially when we were dealing with the African-American community, there would be destruction. The glowing ember was getting brighter and brighter. If we gave into the threat of violence and "let" the African-American people win, the majority would once again bottle up their pride. The anger and rage induced by the feeling of losing would just feed the ember even more next time.

In the United States, we are constantly gathering around an unholy fire of interracial tension, ready to accuse each other—

ready to point the finger, ready to burn over who is winning and who is losing. Many times, like Peter, we avoid the conflict in the name of self preservation, resulting in more suppressed anger and guilt. When we see a fire, our tendency is to run from it. Our instinct is to avoid it. But as Christians, we are asked by God to go against our instinct. With Jesus as our example, we are asked to face the danger and see it as an opportunity in which the presence of God is made known. God, through Jesus Christ, gives us the courage to face the cross, die to our fear, and rise up to meet any challenge. We must transform the unholy, glowing ember into the liberating burning bush. We must sanctify the unholy fire and turn it into the tongues of fire at Pentecost through which the mighty work of God is communicated. In Chinese, the word for "crisis" is a compound word combining the word "danger" and "opportunity." Avoiding the fire is not a solution. By facing the danger of the fire, and by focusing on God's holy presence, we can see opportunities for mutual under-standing, creative reconciling, and peacemaking.

I was invited to speak at an interracial conference in a South-ern state in the fall of 1995. I had prepared a speech a couple of weeks earlier that addressed the power dynamics between Afri-can Americans and European Americans, since I knew that these were the two majority groups at this conference. Four days before the conference, the O. J. Simpson verdict was announced. He was found not guilty. As I observed the reactions from people around me for three days, I realized I had to change my speech. I had a more urgent issue to address because the unholy, glowing ember was getting hotter. In fact, it was flaring up fast. Emotional reactions to the verdict were at two extremes. On the one side, people were angry that Simpson had "gotten away with murder." They blamed the mostly African-American jury for not being willing to convict their own kind. The implication was that African Americans were not to be trusted to achieve justice within our system. This was the reason why "we lost." On the other ex-treme, people reacted with joy and celebration. "He was inno-cent; I knew he was innocent from the start." Many said, "One up for us." The African Americans had won.

Upon arrival at the airport, an African-American woman met me. We were going to have an early supper together, and then she would take to the conference site. After the usual introduc-tion, she confronted me, "So, what do you think? Is he guilty or not?"

I wanted to discuss with her my reaction to the verdict, but this was not the time or place to do it. But her question hung in the air in front of me; what I saw was that our relationship, which had hardly begun, seemed to depend entirely on my answer to this question. What would her reaction be? If I said I didn't believe he was guilty, we would just have a pleasant conversation about how we were on the same winning side. If I said I felt he was guilty, my supper and ride to the conference would be accompanied by more of her proofs of his innocence while my credibility as the speaker of the conference would be conditioned by her review of my "performance." I felt like Peter sitting around an unholy fire ready to flare up. Fingers of right and wrong, good and bad, were ready to rise and point. Whose side are you on?!

My instinct said, "Avoid it. Walk away." But my guilt would overtake me if I did. So where did I find the courage to face the fire? If this incident were any indication of the conference participants' mind-set, I would have to address this sooner or later. I smelled the smoke of the unholy, glowing ember clouding up the atmosphere with a no/yes, either/or, win/lose aura. If I continued on the same track without any act of intervention, this unholy fire would definitely blaze out of control. What would God say in this situation? How could I consecrate this fire and invite God to make it holy? I pondered for half a minute. Then I said, "Do you want an honest answer?"

"Of course," she said.

"I could tell you what you want to hear and then we can have a superficial friendship or I could tell you what I really felt, which would mean that I need you to promise to maintain a dialogue with me."

"What do you mean?"

"No matter what I will say, I need to know that you and I will continue to listen to each other's points of view or I will not want to continue any further."

"Okay."

"At the time the verdict was announced, my immediate reaction was that he was guilty and had gotten off. But...." I hesitated a little; she interrupted.

"How can you think that he was guilty? The gloves didn't fit! They had never...."

"Wait a minute!" I interrupted her this time. "This is exactly what I didn't want to do. You promised that you would maintain a dialogue with me, not to prove that you were right and I was wrong." My heart was pounding because the unholy fire was flaring up. But I continued, "I need you to listen to me until I am finished and then I will invite you to do the same."

She conceded.

"What I was trying to say was that after I recognized my initial reaction to the verdict, I began to ponder on why I felt that way. In the United States, I am supposed to believe the jury. When they say a person is not guilty, then that person is not. But I found myself having a hard time with this one. I asked myself, 'Am I being a racist by feeling that way? What caused me to have this reaction?' Then I realized that I had a really negative reaction to men who abuse their wives. Perhaps that was what I was holding onto, rather than seeing the evidence as the jury saw it. Once I got over that, I was able to understand the jury's perspective. I wish more people would struggle with their reactions to the verdict, whether it was a reaction of joy or anger. But I don't see that anywhere this week. Everybody is taking sides. Nobody is listening. Nobody is communicating with each other."

She listened and then she shared her reaction to the verdict. She also explained why she felt that way. We continued the dialogue all through supper and the ride to the conference site. As we talked and listened to each other, I realized my speech at the conference was going to be okay. I realized the first step to transforming this unholy fire is to move people from the judgmental, win/lose mind-set, to a both/and, nonjudgmental state of mind. This means moving people from being the judge themselves to recognizing God as the ultimate judge. Instead of giving a speech for the time I was given in the conference, I spoke briefly about the issues; then I presented the communication ground rules.[1] I divided the participants into small groups, giving them the opportunity to engage in constructive dialogue. Many participants were grateful to be able to speak about their honest feelings for the first time since the announcement of the verdict. For many of them, this was the first time they heard and understood another point of view without feeling that they had to defend themselves.

As long as we hold on to the win/lose mind-set, the unholy ember will continue to hold us hostage, threatening to flare up and destroy if we do not obey and fall in line with the cycle of destruction. This cycle of destruction consistently forces us into taking sides. The cycle is a ritual dance we perform when we gather around an unholy fire. The choreography goes like this:

If I am on the side of the minority, I feel that I am always losing when I come up against the system. I allow my anger and

---

[1] See Chapter 10 for a full example and full discussion of communication ground rules.

rage to build up. When I cannot contain my anger and rage, I strike back through explosive destruction. When I do, I feel like I have won and the system seems to be a little more open to listening to my needs. But then the system clamps up again later, even tighter than before, and I feel like a loser again.

If I am on the side of the majority, I win by taking control of the system that protects my privileges and rights. I lose when I let the minorities threaten me with their anger, rage, and destruction. When I lose, I strike back with more force to contain the destruction. In my fear of the destruction's reoccurring in the future, I create more control in the system that will favor and protect me. I will not lose again. Each time there is a winner and a loser, this cycle of destruction is energized some more, with the losing side becoming even more determined to win next time.

We are obsessed with this cycle of destruction. We are obsessed with this unholy fire.

As Christians, we must find ways to break this cycle of destruction. We must not allow this unholy fire to cloud up our spirit with fear. We must face the fear, die to the fear, and be resurrected in a new life of hope and new creation. We must break loose from the cycle of destruction by refusing to be cast as sports spectators in the interracial arena, choosing sides. We must refuse the temptation to play God by pronouncing judgment: who is right or wrong, who wins or loses. Instead, we must invite God to enter the unholy fire and sanctify it, transforming it into the burning bush. With God's help, we have the courage to stop needing to win and not be afraid of being called a loser. With God's divine judgment, we stop seeing ourselves as better or worse than the others, but rather regard each other as equals. With God's presence, we can create a holy ground, where people can face each other on level ground, neither winning nor losing. With God's creative power, we can transform the fire from being a destructive, energy-draining, and spirit-dampening force into a creative, empowering, and spirit-filled light.

CHAPTER FIVE

The Golden Calf Syndrome

As we respond to God's call to embrace the burning bush and move toward creating a multicultural community, there will be many uncertainties that we have to deal with, not avoid. There is the uncertainty of meeting others with a different set of values and beliefs, and even a different relationship with God. What if we disagree and start fighting? What would they do to me? If I hold back my judgment, how do I know what is right and what is wrong anymore? Does that mean anything goes? How do I make a moral and ethical decision in a multicultural community? To many people, the idea of developing a multicultural community is like starting a fire. We are afraid of the uncertainties created by this fire; we are fearful that it may flare up and consume us. Our fear and avoidance of this uncertainty is the part of that cycle of destruction that makes us delay having to deal with the conflict directly until it gets so hot that it explodes.

When we do not see the presence of God in our uncertainties, we become fearful of our future. Where are we heading with this messy intercultural web? We see the uncertainties as nothing but chaos and confusion. We yearn for order. We crave something that will assure us of a safe future. We retreat from facing our uncertainty in search of an assurance that we can touch, see, and hear. We fall back onto the safety of pronouncing judgment on others. By judging the others as bad or wrong, we put them in a category that we can safely file away on our orderly arranged mental shelf, and we do not have to deal with them anymore. We fall back on using our technology to build a tower so high that we isolate ourselves from having to deal with anyone who is different. We demand a golden calf around which we can dance our rituals, creating the illusion that we are safe and certain of our future.

> When the people saw that Moses delayed to come down from the mountain, the people gathered around Aaron, and said to him, "Come, make gods for us, who shall go before us; as for this Moses, the man who brought us up out of the land of Egypt, we do not know what has become of him." Aaron said to them, "Take off the gold rings that are on the ears of your wives, your sons, and your daughters, and bring them to me." So all the people took off the gold rings from their ears, and brought them to Aaron. He took the gold from them, formed it in a mold, and cast an image of a calf; and they said, "These are your gods, O Israel, who brought you up out of the land of Egypt!" When Aaron saw this, he built an altar before it; and Aaron made proclamation and said, "Tomorrow shall be a festival to the LORD." They rose early the next day, and offered burnt offerings and brought sacrifices of well-being; and the people sat down to eat and drink, and rose up to revel.
>
> Exodus 32:1–6

In this Exodus story, the people of Israel had left their oppressive, but orderly, lives in Egypt to follow Moses, who led them to Mount Sinai. While Moses was up on the mountain receiving the covenant from God, they began to have doubts about the certainty of their future. Moses, who had been their leader, was gone. They could not see him. They could not hear him. Neither could they see and hear the God on behalf of whom Moses acted. This God had no name or image they could adore. This God had nothing concrete that they could touch or hold in their hand. In their inability to deal with their uncertainty, they forced Aaron to create a golden calf, using their valuable gold earrings. The golden calf was an image that they could see; a statue that they could touch. It would be the god who would lead them out of the wilderness into the land of milk and honey. They performed their ritual dance around this concrete, tangible god, believing that it would bring them certainty for the future.

Uncertainty about the future is a basic fact of life. Human beings are bound by linear time, and have no way of knowing what will happen in the next second until the next second has arrived. We have attempted to predict what will happen in the future using our technologies. We create rules and laws to ensure that our future will be in some kind of civil order. We perform rituals that will make us feel more certain about our future. These rules, technologies, and rituals may have started out as genuine efforts to address uncertainties in people's lives, such as medical technology to heal people who are sick, laws that foster community respect for each other's rights, and rituals for various rites of passage. But they can become golden calves when we allow ourselves to believe that our technologies can enable us to reach up to heaven and become gods ourselves; or that our laws can give us the power to judge others as right or wrong, good or bad; or that our rituals can ensure a definite future for us. They become golden calves when we use them to satisfy our craving for order and are not willing to face the uncertainty that comes with relating to a dynamic, living God.

God insists that we relate to God as a living being, not as a static thing. The movement of God in history had demonstrated that for us to live in a covenant relationship with God was a constant struggle. We kept falling into the "golden calf syndrome" by narrowing and confining God into a static set of rules and rituals. Going back to the Exodus story, God delivered the Israelites out of Egypt—where there were clearly stated rules and roles—and led them into the wilderness, where there were no rigid structure and no rigid rules. God invited the Israelites to have faith in their dynamic relationship with God. "Faith is the assurance of things hoped for, the conviction of things not seen" (Hebrews 11:1). They were asked to live by faith in a God not seen in the face of mounting uncertainties in the wilderness. They were asked to hope for a promised land that was nowhere in sight in the desert. Their human need for certainty and assurance was so great that even God gave into it.

When the Israelites could not deal with not having any rules, God transformed his covenant with Israel into a set of laws—the commandments. These commandments were meant to be living laws interpreting their relationship with God. God gave the commandments, but insists that the covenant was more important. However, the people made the laws into the golden calf, instead, and worshiped these rules, using them to judge others as if the law were God. The attitude of the Pharisees depicted in the Christian Scriptures was a prime example of how we take something that was meant to be dynamic and make it into a static set of oppressive and exclusive rules and rituals.

With the coming of Jesus, God once again tried to emphasize the covenant and not the rules or rituals. "Do not think that I have come to abolish the law or the prophets; I have come not to abolish but to fulfill" (Matthew 5:17). To fulfill the law was to recapture the relationship with God—the covenant. Jesus talked about the essential commandments—love God and love your neighbor, and "on these two commandments hang all the law and the prophets" (Matthew 22:40). In the process of recapturing the covenant relationship with God, Jesus also reinterpreted the rigid laws. Some of the well-known ones are those regarding divorce and anger. But then we took these reinterpretations of the law that were meant to recapture the relationship with God, and made them into the golden calf. Divorce is absolutely sinful; Jesus said so. Having angry thoughts is a sin; Jesus said so. We use scripture in the same limiting way. The Bible said this and it is the absolute truth and we must believe it and follow it. But we are forgetting the Bible is the record of God's action in human history. It is a living document that helps us recapture again and again our covenant with God. We cannot use the Bible as a golden calf, turning it into a static set of rules. The law, the sayings of Jesus, and the Bible as a written document are not all there is to God. They are but expressions of the living covenantal relationship we have with God through Jesus Christ.

However, the golden calf syndrome is very strong, and we are naturally drawn to it, because uncertainty in life is a constant challenge to us. Our human survival instinct would steer us toward the golden calf syndrome if we did not intervene and redirect our focus in our covenantal relationship with God. Let us examine further how we use technologies, rules, and rituals as golden calves, to avoid uncertainty.[1] We will explore how they help us avoid uncertainties in general, and then we will survey how we use them to avoid the uncertainty of moving toward a multicultural community.

Technology in general helps us avoid the uncertainty created by nature. For example, when it rained in ages past and we did not like the uncertainty of developing a cold, we invented the technology of making an umbrella to keep us dry. If we wanted to get to the other side of a river where there were trees with sweet, ripe fruits, we invented the technology of building a bridge or a boat so that we could avoid the uncertainty of not finding food. We currently use satellite technology to predict

---

[1] Using technology, rules, and rituals as avoidance strategies is used by Geert Hofstede to describe the cultural variable he called "Uncertainty Avoidance." See Geert Hofstede, *Culture's Consequences—International Differences in Work-Related Values,* abridged edition (Beverly Hills, London, New Delhi: Sage Publications, 1987), pp. 110–147.

weather in order to alleviate many environmental uncertainties. Our whole medical technology is built upon this avoidance of uncertainty created by diseases for which we may or may not find the cure. Technologies give us the illusion that we can conquer nature. They give us the illusion that we can create anything, build anything—just as if we were gods ourselves. The story of the Tower of Babel is a biblical example of how the technology of making bricks and building with them caused people to believe they could build a tower to reach the heavens and make a name for themselves.

We also use technology to avoid the uncertainty created by human behavior. For example, because we did not like the uncertainty created by the threat of another country's military power, we developed technology for more destructive weapons, such as the nuclear bomb, to "protect" us. Whether these technologies actually protect us is another question, but having them makes us feel safer. Ironically, the technology of the video camera was supposed to create the certainty that Rodney King was going to get justice not only for himself but for the whole African-American community. Many African Americans would say, "Before this happened, nobody would believe us when we complained about how the police had beaten us up for no reason at all. It's the policeman's words against ours. Now we have solid proof." But when this technology did not help, we became more outraged. Why? Because technology was our golden calf. We trusted it to give us justice rather than trusting God. Technology, when it becomes the golden calf, will have the opposite effect in the long run. It will simply feed the unholy fire, fanning it some more, and preparing it to explode at a later day.

Using technology to avoid uncertainty is inextricably linked with money. The more money you have, the more technologies you can buy to alleviate uncertainties in your life. We will sacrifice a great deal of our wealth in order to find assurance in our lives. "The people took off the gold rings from their ears and brought them to Aaron." I was attending a conference on multiculturalism for educators in California. One of the workshops was on technology. The speaker asked the participants to share why they chose to attend this workshop. One of the responses was, "I think technology is the answer to the problem of multiculturalism that we are facing in the classroom. If we have a computer for each student and the student can learn everything by interacting with the computer, then they don't have to interact with students from other cultures." This response is a real example of how we avoid intercultural uncertainty by utilizing technology. I have known institutions that would spend a large sum of money to buy the most advanced computer systems, truly believing that this technology will help them address every issue and conflict in the organization.

I was consulting with a church that had been exclusively English-speaking and the majority of the membership were European Americans. This church was supported by a major endowment and a number of very wealthy families who had moved away from the neighborhood but still commuted to church. Meanwhile, more and more Korean-American residents moved into the neighborhood surrounding the church. There was some effort on the leadership's part in dealing with the changing demographics. They had hired a part-time Korean pastor who would help them deal with the needs of the Korean community. When I asked them why they hired him as only a part-time pastor, the response was, "We don't have enough funding to get a full-time person." As I left the church, I saw major construction next to the church building. I asked the senior pastor what was going on. He said that they were building a brand new parish hall as part of their revitalization of the community. Last year, they had also bought and installed a very expensive organ for the church. It was, in his perception, an offering to the community.

As I drove away from the church, I observed the Korean signs on the storefronts, block after block. I thought to myself, "Our technologies that give us the ability to build magnificent edifices and wonderful-sounding organs have become a golden calf for this church." Instead of spending their resources on developing the human ability to relate to each other across the cultural barrier, they spent their resources on things and technologies that they could see, hear, and touch. Technology gave them the illusion that they were doing something about the issues, but in reality, they were avoiding the issues all along.

Rules are our way of addressing uncertainty created by human behavior. In order to avoid the uncertainty of being robbed when we walked down the street, we created a law that made robbery a crime, and those who committed this crime would be punished. In order to avoid the uncertainty of being run down by a car while crossing the street, we created a set of driving rules that everyone had to know by passing a driving test before they could get a license to drive. In order to avoid the uncertainty of physicians' making mistakes with our lives, we created a legal system by which we could sue a physician for malpractice. Even though by the time one sues, the damage has already been done, by having such a system, we believe doctors will be more careful.

Again, these rules may or may not directly address the uncertainty, but they provide us with a level of comfort in the face of uncertainty. It is ironic that while the United States values individual freedom, it has such an elaborate legal system with volumes and volumes of laws. Individual freedom means less control over the individual's behavior. But this freedom, by nature, creates more uncertainty for everyone. So we compensate by creating more laws that are supposed to control people's freedom to behave.

Having rules gives us a sense of order and safety. When we attempt to create a multicultural community, we will be facing the confusion of having more than one set of deeply held values and beliefs. The relativity of these systems of thoughts and assumptions can make us feel like there is no solid ground to stand on anymore. In our fear of chaos, we jump to the conclusion that we need more rules. If only we can make them behave the way we do, we will be able to live together in harmony. Instead of engaging others in dialogue and negotiation, we dismiss them with our rules by judging them as wrong. Instead of trusting God to help us live through the uncertainty, we build a golden calf of rules and regulations that fence others off, creating an illusion that we are safe and protected.

In a multicultural dialogue session in Hawaii, a Samoan member of a church got up to share some of his thoughts and perceptions about the intercultural relationship with the *haole* in his church. (*Haole* is a native Hawaiian term for non-Hawaiians.) He said, "We are a people who believe church is the extension of the family. When we are in church, we want our children to behave like they are at home. So sometimes they run around the church during the service, and they play in the kitchen and the parish hall. But the English-speaking congregation was complaining about our children being out of control. Sometimes I feel like they care more about the spoon in their kitchen than about the children."

The *haole* group was shocked. They had no idea that the Samoans felt that way about the new rules that they had posted in the parish hall that said, "No Running." Instead of relating to the people who behaved differently, the *haole* chose to avoid the issue with a golden calf: Here is the new rule. To truly be a multicultural community, we cannot rely on rules and regulations to force others to behave as we want. By imposing our values onto others, we pronounce judgment—they are wrong if they don't follow our rules. Rules, then, become our way of avoiding dialogue and constructive interaction, whereby we try to understand each other's differences and negotiate for a common set of ground rules by which everyone in the community could live and affirm.

Another church with which I was working had experienced a 30 percent drop in membership in six months. The church members who left were the ones who wanted contemporary music in worship. When they encountered resistance to change from the rest of the congregation, they gathered together and insisted on designing a worship service that would be to their liking. Furthermore, they insisted that this service be on Sunday morning. When they finally held the contemporary-music service, they did not receive overwhelming approval from the majority of the congregation. Very few people came up to them and said, "Let's do this every Sunday from now on." The organizers of the service did not take the reactions of a few positive people and stay to build upon that support; instead they decided to listen to what they considered to be the negative reactions of the rest of the congregation. So they got mad and left with no negotiation, and no attempt at dialogue. They just left.

When we want to avoid conflicts, we create rules in our heads—rules that say this is the right way and that is the wrong way. When these rules are in place, there is no room for dialogue, which eliminates the possibility of interacting with others who believe differently. With these rules, we judge, we believe we are right, and we play God—one more ritual dance around the golden calf lighting up the unholy fire.

When rules and technologies have failed to provide us with the certainty that we need, most people turn to ritual. Each cultural group has its traditions in providing rituals for the most uncertain times of people's lives—birth, coming of age, marriage, death, and others. At a time of illness we have rituals of spiritual healing, anointing with oil, and prayer groups. When I was young and ill a lot of the time, my mother and I had this ritual. She would pray next to my bed, and then she formed a cross with two toothpicks and placed it under my mattress. It did not matter whether those toothpicks were going to make me well or not; I felt better, and I did believe that I was going to be better the next day. Many rituals like this one do not deal directly with the uncertainty being faced; the ritual has more of a psychological effect.

Rituals in organizations are just as prevalent, even though most of the time we do not recognize them as rituals. For example, when a church organization was facing the uncertainty of racial conflicts, a typical ritual would be to form a study committee which, as an end result, would usually put out a report. Many denominations had shelves of these reports. Each one raised the same issues and concerns. These reports were often done about every three to five years. The study committee may or may not address the issue of racial conflict constructively, but by the act of starting such a committee, the organization believed that it was doing something about this uncertainty that they were facing. Another ritual was to hire an expert and let the expert take care of the problem. Again, the "expert" may or may not be an expert at all. Sometimes the expert was not given enough time to address the issue in depth. But by going through the ritual, the leaders and some of the members of the organization felt that the issue was being addressed. Many of these rituals, if followed through, do turn into successful strategies that address the uncertainty directly. Unfortunately, in many of the cases, as soon as the ritual was in place, people felt more at ease and therefore stopped pursuing the important follow-up activities that dealt with issues in concrete ways.

A diocese invited me to design and facilitate a three-month long interracial dialogue program that would involve at least ten congregations of different cultural backgrounds. I met with the bishop, and the bishop, against my recommendations, decided to start a committee that would oversee this process. I met with the committee, and the committee decided to set up a process that would involve testing out the preliminary design of the dialogue program with the bishop's staff in a one-day event. Based on the responses to this one-day event, I would refine the process further and then train facilitators to execute this program for the congregations in the diocese. We had scheduled a date for this one-day event, but as we moved closer to the day, they realized that too many people had decided at the last minute to take vacation time. So we picked another date three months down the road—plenty of time for everyone to clear their calendars. One week before this date, I was in a meeting with this committee to finalize the logistics of this one-day dialogue event. One member of the committee said very seriously, "I don't think we should do the interracial dialogue now because we are not ready for it. One of our staff members just got fired and the rest of the staff is still dealing with this."

"But this dialogue process will deal with this as well as interracial issues," I argued. "That is what dialogue is about. We can deal with any issue as it comes up."

"No," another member of the committee said, "I don't think we can deal with this and the interracial problem. That would be too confusing."

After a few more rounds of this pattern of argument, I finally realized that I was dealing with a ritual that this group was performing. By performing this ritual, they were avoiding having to deal with interracial issues for themselves. Furthermore, this ritual was delaying the whole diocese's interracial dialogue program. Finally, a good friend on the committee who also saw what was going on said, "Eric, why don't we forget this committee and the bishop's staff? Why don't you and the bishop figure out how to get this dialogue program going for the congregations? I don't think it's fair for you to wait for us to get ready to do this."

With this, the committee reluctantly disbanded itself and I was free to implement the dialogue program. I was fortunate to have broken away from this ritual and was able to move forward with this project. Many organizations, both secular and religious, never move beyond this ritual that they perform when dealing with intercultural issues. How many resolutions have we passed in our denominational meetings regarding racial justice? How many studies have we done to examine the issues of racism? If these resolutions (rules) and studies (ritual) are not followed by actual human contact in constructive dialogue and actions, they are just a ritual dance that we do around the golden calf.

Technologies, rules, and rituals are not by nature evil. However, they have the potential to become golden calves if we use them to avoid the uncertainties of intercultural human encounters, without which a multicultural community is impossible to build. God, through Jesus Christ, invites us to enter courageously into the uncertain wilderness of interracial relations. God calls us to step out of the safety of our rules and technologies and rituals and face the uncertainty of meeting others who are different. In God's multicultural community, there must not be any golden calves. We must enable each other to let go of our golden calves before we enter the multicultural community. We must transform the ritual that we perform into liturgy that gathers around the burning bush. We must learn to utilize technologies in the context of a liturgy. We must sanctify technology so that it is truly an extension of our real selves that can reach out across language and cultural barriers and touch others with our honesty and receive others with open channels of communication. We must convert our absolute, judgmental rules and laws into a true expression of our covenant with others and with God. We must remember that it is not the static rules and rituals that make us a holy people, but our dynamic, living relationship with God that makes us a holy people who can face any uncertainty as we develop our multicultural community.

CHAPTER SIX

Up and Down the Tower of Babel: Another Vision of a Multicultural Community

I was doing a three-day multicultural leadership training event for a group of lay and ordained ministers. In the afternoon of the second day, after I had covered the foundational material, a hand rose up from the back of the room. A challenging voice asked, "Why are we doing this?" I was surprised by this question because my perception was that this group was appreciating the material I had presented so far. The majority of the participants echoed my reaction with their body language. Some even went further in sending out signals of displeasure and judgment against the speaker. "That's a stupid question!" one participant retorted.

But it was not a stupid question, no matter what the speaker intended to do with his question. This question challenged me to examine my assumption that learning to develop a multicultural community is good. Why is it good? Hasn't our history shown us enough pain, conflict, and destruction when people of different racial and ethnic backgrounds collide with each other? Are we not flirting with disaster in our desire to create a multicultural community? Are we not falling into the trap of repeating history and adding more ugly, destructive episodes to the already long list of destructive interracial incidents? Haven't we had enough? Why bother to create and develop a multicultural community? Is it not easier and more comfortable to worship in the language, custom, and style with which we are most accustomed? Isn't it easier and more efficient to discuss and share our ministry in a common context and language? Perhaps it is better to be separate, to avoid having contact with each other. Maybe that is the only way we can have peace. The question "Why are we doing this?" challenges the core value of my ministry. It was a question that I had to answer. As I attempted to answer the question at this training event, I found myself telling the story of the Tower of Babel.

> Now the whole earth had one language and the same words. And as they migrated from the east, they came upon a plain in the land of Shinar and settled there. And they said to one another, "Come, let us make bricks, and burn them thoroughly." And they had brick for stone, and bitumen for mortar. Then they said, "Come, let us build ourselves a city, and a tower with its top in the heavens, and let us make a name for ourselves; otherwise we shall be scattered abroad upon the face of the whole earth." The LORD came down to see the city and the tower, which mortals had built. And the LORD said, "Look, they are one people, and they have all one language; and this is only the beginning of what they will do; nothing that they propose to do will now be impossible for them. Come, let us go down, and confuse their language there, so that they will not understand one another's speech." So the LORD scattered them abroad from there over the face of all the earth and they left off building the city. Therefore it was called Babel, because there the LORD confused the language of all the earth; and from there the LORD scattered them abroad over the face of all the earth.
>
> Genesis 11:1–9

Why did God want to confuse their language so that they couldn't communicate with one another? What did God want to accomplish? Is this ancient story telling us that God intentionally did not want us to understand each other? Is this story telling us that God did not want us to be one people? Wouldn't this story support segregation? Before we draw such fast conclusions, let us first consider what these people were doing that was offensive to God while they were speaking one language. Maybe we will discover why God took such a drastic action.

As a people with one language, they were trying to build a city and a tower with its top in the heavens and they wanted to make a name for themselves. In the convenience of one language and culture, they became so sure of themselves to the point that they believed they could reach heaven through their technology—brick for stone, and bitumen for mortar. They began to think of themselves as becoming gods who could live in heaven and had a name for others to worship. In their confidence in their ability, they forgot that they were humankind created by God. This is the offense that God was trying to address. In their monolingual culture, they forgot who God was.

Once again, we find a recurring theme in scripture—God's being angry at humankind's attempts to become like gods themselves. God's action of "confusing their language" had to address this issue of adultery. By confusing their language, God was trying to remind them who God was. But how did the inability to communicate with one another help us to understand God better? The scattering of people all over the face of the earth was only the beginning of this process of the purification of our sins. To complete this process, God through Jesus Christ challenged us to move toward Pentecost, where people of different languages and cultures were finally communicating with each other, but for the purpose of showing the mighty works of God. As we struggle to reach Pentecost, overcoming intercultural barriers, we are forced to recognize that each cultural group, with its unique context, experiences God differently. In our intercultural dialogue, we compare these different experiences of God. We realize that God is not confined by our culture. Instead, God moves in and alongside each culture to challenge and affirm each according to its strengths and weaknesses. In this realization, we are better able to separate our cultures and our languages from God's culture and language. In the process of our struggle to communicate across cultural and language barriers, we see more clearly who God is in our lives and ministries, which was what God set out to do at the Tower of Babel when God confused our language.

The story of the early church's struggling with its identity provided an example of this process of discerning God through intercultural dialogue. The community of Gentile believers in Antioch was established by Paul and Barnabas. As this community grew, there were questions about what was required of the Gentile believers, since up to that point, the majority of the believers had their roots in the Jewish tradition. Paul and Barnabas took the responsibility to bring the concerns of the Antioch community back to Jerusalem. They engaged in dialogue on this "hot" topic with the community in Jerusalem.

> But some believers who belonged to the sect of the Pharisees stood up and said, "It is necessary for them to be circumcised and ordered to keep the law of Moses." The

apostles and the elders met together to consider this matter. After there had been much debate, Peter stood up and
said to them, "My brothers, you know that in the early
days God made a choice among you, that I should be the
one through whom the Gentiles would hear the message
of the good news and become believers. And God, who
knows the human heart, testified to them by giving them
the Holy Spirit, just as he did to us; and in cleansing their
hearts by faith he has made no distinction between them
and us. Now therefore why are you putting God to the test
by placing on the neck of the disciples a yoke that neither
our ancestors nor we have been able to bear? On the con-
·trary, we believe that we will be saved through the grace
of the Lord Jesus, just as they will."

Acts 15:5–11

Later a letter was drafted, and Paul and Barnabas, along with
Judas and Silas, sent by the Jerusalem community, delivered the
letter to the Antioch community. It said:

"For it has seemed good to the Holy Spirit and to us to
impose on you no further burden than these essentials:
that you abstain from what has been sacrificed to idols
and from blood and from what is strangled and from forni-
cation. If you keep yourselves from these, you will do well.
Farewell."

Acts 15:28–29

The dispute was over whether Christianity could be built on a
context other than that of the Jewish foundation. The resolution
was that the Christian faith, the context of God as defined by
Jesus, did not necessarily require the Jewish context. This meant
that the Jewish believers could continue to practice what they
believed to be important to them and the Gentile believers could
also do the same according to their own traditions as long as they
maintained and practiced what was *essential* to being a believer
of Jesus. In this early church dialogue, they redefined or purified
their vision of what it meant to be a believer, to be a part of the
Christian community. Furthermore, they discovered that the gospel was independent of their cultural values. The gospel challenged each culture differently according to the disparity between that culture's values and God's values. In this separation of
their culture and God's culture, they determined what were the
essentials of their faith; they saw God more clearly.

The Gentile believers in the early church were a prophetic voice that enabled the larger community to see a purer vision of God's culture. In this intercultural dispute, the fire was burning. The easy way to avoid this conflict was to hold fast to the Jewish rituals and rules as absolutes that every believer had to follow, eliminating the need to discuss or negotiate. The fire had the potential to consume and exclude, but with dialogue and the acknowledgment of the presence of God in each cultural group, the fire was made holy and served as a purifying agent. This was a burning-bush community that did not consume others as they dealt with hot topics. It is most appropriate that "it was in Antioch that the disciples were first called 'Christians'" (Acts 11:26). Their prophetic role helped the early church define and refine its identity. This is the essence of why I believe developing a multicultural community is so important to the life of the church. In a multicultural community, we encounter people of different cultural backgrounds in constructive ways. We sanctify the fire of interracial conflict and use it to purify our vision of God and of ourselves as a Christian community. Encountering a group of another culture with a different experience of God facilitates the divine judgment. The differing other becomes the prophet who pronounces the judgment of God, making us realize that we are not God. In doing so, our vision of God is clarified and purified. Our perception of community is more complete and more faithful.

If the early Christian community had decided that the only way to be a believer was to become Jewish first, Christianity would not exist as we know it now. Christianity would simply be a sect of Judaism. The decision to move from a dispute over an "either–or" solution to a "both–and" resolution set the precedent for the rest of Christian history in the centuries that followed. In the search to be closer to God, we made the separation between the gospel and the Jewish culture from which it sprung. This does not mean that Judaism is not valid anymore. The Jewish community, apart from the development of Christianity, continued to respond to God in its culturally specific and challenging way up to the present. But as Christians, we have a special calling put forth by Jesus Christ, to be God's witnesses "in Jerusalem, in all Judea and Samaria, and to the ends of the earth" (Acts 1:8). We are called to engage in intercultural dialogue through which we can see God more clearly apart from our own culture. We are called again and again to discern what the "essentials" of the gospel are as we share and compare our faith and culture with others who are different. While I accept that the gospel has to express itself through the specifics of each culture, and that it is very hard to separate the gospel from our culture, I believe that it is through the struggle to discern the gospel apart from our culture that drives us to continuously discern the will of God more faithfully.

> As a deer longs for flowing streams,
> > so my soul longs for you, O God.
> My soul thirsts for God,
> > for the living God.
> When shall I come and behold
> > the face of God?
> > > Psalm 42:1–2

I was facilitating a bilingual, interracial dialogue for a church that I will call St. Paul's Church. St. Paul's had been an English-speaking church exclusively until three years ago, when the leadership decided to start a Spanish-language worship and ministry because of the rapid growth of the Spanish-speaking community around the neighborhood. Six months prior to the dialogue event, the church leadership heard more and more complaints from the English-speaking members regarding the inappropriate conduct of the Spanish-speaking members. Furthermore, they complained that the Spanish-speaking members did not speak up when there was a problem until it was too late. Some referred to the Spanish-speaking community as "passive-aggressive."

As part of the dialogue process, I invited the participants to complete the sentence: "Church is _____." Most of the responses from the English-speaking participants were individualized definitions of church. Here is a sampling of their responses:

"Church is a community of people who worship together."
"Church is a place where I find people with the same conviction for ministry."
"Church is the body of Christ."
"Church is where I participate in the community of God."

As we observed what the Spanish-speaking participants wrote, we began to realize the difference in perception and understanding of the definition of church. Most of the Spanish-speaking responses were the same: "Church is St. Paul's."

"But what does that mean?" asked an English-speaking participant. "St. Paul's can be many things to different people." As they spoke, the English-speaking participants expressed an attitude that said if St. Paul's evolved into something else other than their definition of church, they, as individuals, could choose to leave and search out another church that would better fit their definition of "church."

The questions and responses coming from the English-speaking participants surprised the Spanish-speaking participants. They could not comprehend initially why the English-speaking participants took church so lightly. To them, "church" was St. Paul's, no matter what St. Paul's was, is, or will be tomorrow. They came to church because St. Paul's was their church. St. Paul's was part of their reality, part of their collective—somewhat like an extension of their family in the sense that one could not deny a family member, no matter how you felt about that person.

Moving deeper into the dialogue, the Spanish-speaking participants began to understand why the English-speaking members of the church were so threatened by the thriving Spanish-language community: the presence of the Spanish-speaking members was changing the definition of St. Paul's. The English-speaking members may have felt that they were losing their church, and they might have to leave. On the other hand, the English-speaking participants began to understand why the Spanish-speaking church members did not speak up when there was a problem because they wanted to maintain harmonious relations with everyone in the church, including the English-speaking members.

With this mutual understanding, they arrived at a fuller understanding of what a church community was about. It was about a sense of collective identity, like a family, as well as respecting different individuals' dreams and visions that may challenge the tradition of the community. In the dynamics of the inertia of tradition, and the prophetic challenges of the individual dreams and visions, the church moved, evolved, and grew, becoming more faithful to its calling and more faithful to the community it serves.

St. Paul's had achieved physical inclusion by opening its doors to the Spanish-speaking community, but without creating opportunities for the English-speaking and Spanish-speaking groups to engage in constructive dialogue, the conflict between the two groups escalated without both sides intending to do so. The dialogue experience was the first step for St. Paul's to move toward a truly respectful multicultural community. The community of St. Paul's must continue to create such opportunities for constructive dialogue among the different cultural groups across the various language and cultural barriers.

As I discussed in my previous book, *The Wolf Shall Dwell with the Lamb,* inviting two or more different cultural groups to come together in the same space does not make a multicultural community. It is only the first step. Constructive dialogue must follow. If not, the result will be a communications breakdown, and increased inter-group conflicts, because without the dialogue process—the burning bush—each group will build its individual towers, making itself more secure and more like gods to the others.

Our tower of Babel is our ethnocentricism. Ethnocentricism is the belief that our cultural values and beliefs, both conscious and unconscious, are the best and that we possess the superior culture. In our separateness, we build our towers with our unspoken assumptions, values, and beliefs. As the tower gets taller and taller, we create more distance and separation from others who are different. Up in our tower, we create our own rituals that give us the illusion of certainty. Up in the imaginary security of our tower, we may conclude that our culture is God's culture—which, in turn, may lead us to believe that we are gods. When we encounter others who are different, with their own tower, we put them down, call them names, and we stop communicating with them. We judge them as if we are gods. Many churches spent so much energy in building this tower that they lost touch with what was going on in their changing communities on the ground. One day they realized their church was almost empty, with a few aging members. They looked around in the hollow space and wondered what had happened. How did people abandon the tower when it was so beautiful and magnificent?

The first step toward becoming a multicultural community is to recognize our own tower of Babel—our ethnocentrism. Each cultural group has a tendency to make itself superior, believing that its tower is better and taller, and can reach the heavens. In a multicultural community, we need to identify our tower of Babel and decide to consciously stop building it. We need to come down from our tower and see the others on level ground, because as long as we are high up in our own tower, we will be looking down upon others who are lower and competing with those whose towers are taller. As we climb down from our tower, we examine each brick and wall, learning how we got that high. When we finally land—with a fuller consciousness and acceptance of who we are—we are ready to encounter others who also have come down from their towers. On level ground, we keep ourselves in check; we are not better or worse than the others, we are just different. On level ground, we become prophets to each other, challenging each other to see God more clearly and to act more faithfully. On level ground, we can achieve Pentecost, where we prophesy to each other and listen to each other with open ears.

> Then afterward I will pour out my Spirit on all flesh; your sons and your daughters shall prophesy, your old men shall dream dreams, and your young men shall see visions. Even on the male and female slaves, in those days, I will pour out my Spirit.
>
> Joel 2:28–29 (Acts 2:17–18)

But the process continues; it is not a one-time deal. On level ground, we can get frustrated that we cannot seem to build anything together. We can become restless and tired, because we are not in our towers where we can be at ease with people who share the same values, beliefs, and contexts, and where we can talk to each other in our own language. We have to admit that we are not perfect and that we cannot live in Pentecost all the time. So we return to our towers, knowing that the work is not done and we have not fully realized Pentecost. At the same time we must also affirm that we have made some constructive steps in coming down from our towers. As we return to our towers, we see our tower with new eyes. In our separateness, again, we share what we have learned from the intercultural encounter. We gain a prophetic vision and turn our energy to the direction of God, rather than ourselves. We may discover that there are many good gifts, resources, and talents that we used as bricks and mortar to build the tower. We may decide to destroy our tower and use our material to build something else that is more in line with God's wish.

Yet the refining process continues. As human beings, we forget easily. After a period of time, we may have forgotten the prophetic voices that we heard on level ground and start building our tower, reaching for heaven again. That is when we need to look at our towers again, climb down from them, and meet on level ground in order to encounter the prophetic others. Soon, we will return again to our towers to redistribute our resources more faithfully. It is in the climbing down and up and then down our tower of ethnocentrism that we gain new insight into what it means to live in a multicultural community. It is in the building and abandoning of our towers of Babel repeatedly that we encounter God more fully. In the midst of the numerous unfinished towers, we remain horizontal; we remain on the same level, face-to-face with each other, learning from each other, struggling with each other, and challenging each other to be more faithful to God. In this seeming scatteredness—in our different values, dif-

ferent assumptions, different visions, different dreams, and different prophecies—we find the city of God. In the landscape of
abandoned and ruined towers, we come together around the
burning bush again and again, forming and refining a true
multicultural community.

CHAPTER SEVEN

Coming Down from Our Tower of Babel: Examining Our Ethnocentrism

One of the major barriers to building a multicultural community is our ethnocentrism. Ethnocentrism is the assumption that the worldview of one's own culture is central to all reality. In our ethnocentrism, we perceive and evaluate persons, things, and events according to our values, beliefs, and assumptions, often not knowing or accepting other worldviews as valid or important. When we are ethnocentric, we may react with denial to others who have a different cultural worldview, we may become defensive and judgmental, and we may minimize the differences as unimportant. Ethnocentrism is the tower of Babel that each cultural group builds, resulting in the inability to communicate and relate to persons of another culture.

In order to learn how to climb down from our towers of ethnocentrism, we must first learn how to recognize our ethnocentrism. How do I know I am being ethnocentric? What does it feel like? What does it sound like? Then we must learn why we maintain our ethnocentrism. It is only in understanding and accepting the cause of our ethnocentrism that we can move beyond it. In this chapter I will describe seven ethnocentric responses to cultural differences. These responses are by no means inclusive of all possible ethnocentric responses, but they will provide us with behavioral indications with which we can assess our level of intercultural sensitivity. Much of the material in this chapter is based on Milton J. Bennett's intercultural sensitivity developmental model, which focuses on a person's response to difference as an indicator of the stages of intercultural sensitivity development.[1] His theory describes the different stages that one moves through when one is interacting with a culture other than one's own. In addition to using Bennett's description of the ethnocentric stages of his theory, I also added my own observations of other ethnocentric behaviors and responses from my work in churches and higher-education institutions. These seven responses are arranged more or less in their progressive developmental order.

1. Difference does not exist.

We can observe this ethnocentric reaction or nonreaction in young children whose experience of difference is so limited that they don't see any. And if they do see any difference, they might unconsciously ignore it and continue to believe that there is no difference. Sometimes, this attitude continues into adulthood. For example, a person went to Japan on vacation. Upon returning to the United States, he described his experience excitedly. "Japan's wonderful. It's just like America. It has McDonald's, Coca-Cola, and everybody speaks English there." We know this person's observation is incorrect. However, people in their isolation tend to see only what they want to see, often ignoring the most obvious differences.

Social, economical, and physical barriers that isolate groups of people are the cause of these first ethnocentric responses to difference. People who deny that there are differences have often been living in isolation. For example, a newborn baby does not see the difference between herself and her mother. A young child initially does not recognize the difference between male and female. Socially, we all grew up in the isolation of our home life and did not readily see differences until we were exposed to other children with a different home life. If we lived in a homogeneous

---

[1] Bennett organized his theory in six states: Denial, Defense, Minimization, Acceptance, Adaptation, and Integration. Each state is further divided into two or three stages. For this chapter, the description of the ethnocentric responses follows fairly closely to the first three states of Bennett's theory. For a full description of Bennett's theory, see Milton J. Bennett, "A Developmental Approach to Training for Intercultural Sensitivity," in *Theories and Methods in Cross-Cultural Orientation,* ed. Judith N. Martin, International Journal of Intercultural Relations, Vol. 5, No. 2 (New York/Oxford/Beijing/Frankfurt/Sao Paulo/Sydney/Tokyo/Toronto: Pergamon Press, 1986), pp.179–196 and Milton J. Bennett, "Towards Ethnorelativism: A Developmental Model of Intercultural Sensitivity," in *Cross-Cultural Orientation,* ed. R. Michael Paige (Lanham, Maryland: University Press of America, 1986), pp. 27–69.

community where each household in the neighborhood mirrored the others, our isolation continued into an older age, even when we started school. Many of us did not come out of isolation until we pursued higher education or moved to another community for work.

2. Difference is confined to broad categories.

One time after I gave a speech at a large conference, a person approached me with a big smile and asked, "Do you know my friend John from Japan? You look just like him."

"But I'm not from Japan, and I'm not Japanese. I'm Chinese." I replied.

This person then said, "But Chinese, Japanese, what's the difference? They're both Asians."

People with this kind of response to difference cannot distinguish the finer differences among large categories of people. By putting people into broad categories, they acknowledge that there are different people in the world but only at a minimal level. Here we sit on the top of our ethnocentric tower. We feel safe as long as the differing others are perceived also to be confined to their towers at a distance. As long as you are there in your neat little category and I am here, I remain protected.

An African-American woman I interviewed for my research remembered her experience of this response to difference. "Growing up in the South, there was only black and white. We had doctors with Jewish names but we were not really consciously aware of the fact that they were Jewish. And there was a Mr. Rodríguez who owned a candy store. Because he was in a black neighborhood, as far as we were concerned, he was black. We went to school with Puerto Ricans, whom we just assumed were black and so because our world was black-and-white, there weren't these distinctions about Jews and Italians and Puerto Ricans. You were either black or you were white."

This perception of difference was reinforced by intentional separation of groups through physical or social barriers, creating distance, and avoiding contact with different cultural groups. In Los Angeles where I lived and worked for many years, the physical and social barriers that shield people from cultural difference are everywhere. Take a bird's-eye view of the greater Los Angeles area and you will see a mosaic of neighborhoods separated by the cement of class and race. There is Chinatown; Little Saigon; Koreatown; East Los Angeles, which is mostly a Hispanic area; South Central Los Angeles, which is a large black neighborhood; and, of course, the ever-famous Beverly Hills. We believe that if we build walls around different cultural groups, put them in broad categories, and give them labels, then we can put them at a safe distance so that they will not affect our lives.

We also use technology as a golden calf that we can buy to maintain our separation. For example, people who own cars can maintain their isolation in choosing to go only to places that are familiar to them. As a result, some people who were born in a racially mixed city might seldom meet other people of different economic and racial backgrounds for most of their childhood. At the University of Southern California, where I used to work as a campus minister, a student could spend four years going to school there but never really know anybody who lived in the mostly low-income African-American and Spanish-speaking neighborhoods in the surrounding area. On weekends, the university provided a shuttle-bus service that would take students from the USC campus to Westwood, an affluent college-town neighborhood next to UCLA. The university administrators believed that this was their way of providing students with entertainment. This is an example of an institution's reinforcing social barriers and therefore contributing to maintaining the dominant culture's state of denial.

When we are in denial, we hold fast to our golden calves in order to avoid the uncertainty of dealing with people who are different. In our maintenance of our isolation and insulation, we put others in neatly arranged categories that we can touch and hold and put away, and thereby distance ourselves from them. Instead of bowing down to the golden calf that keeps us separate in our towers of denial, we must invite people of different cultures to break these barriers. In so doing, we can help people recognize that there are differences. This is not an easy task. Most of the efforts I have seen have been the artificial "cultural" activities, such as "Mexican Night," the International Food Fair, and ethnic dance performances. Most of these kinds of programs were no more than mere entertainment.

For people who exhibit the first two kinds of ethnocentric responses, I believe some kind of "forced" cross-cultural contact across the separation barriers is necessary, but it has to be done with commitment from the groups involved and with great care from the leadership. Nonthreatening events such as "cultural nights" and the sharing of ethnic food are appropriate, but we must not let it end at the entertainment level. In order for this kind of program to be effective in helping people to climb down from their ethnocentric towers, they must also show participants that there are differences not only among broad categories of cultural groups, but also differences within large ethnic and linguistic categories. For example, if you are organizing a Hispanic or Latino cultural celebration, spotlight the various groups such as the Mexican, Puerto Rican, Salvadoran, Cuban, Costa Rican, Guatemalan, etc., that make up the Latino group. If you are organizing a "white" cultural celebration, be sure to include the French, English, German, Italian, Irish, Norwegian, Slovenian, Russian, and so forth, as well as second-, third-, and fourth-generation European Americans. Reports and lectures on experiences in different ethnic neighborhoods and churches are appropriate. If you allow discussion, be sure that it is monitored by an experienced intercultural dialogue facilitator, because any more in-depth movement will lead to the emergence of defensive behavior, which denotes increased tension. Perhaps the groups involved should be forewarned about negative feelings and tension that might come, and should be invited to make a commitment to see themselves through it.

3. You are different; therefore you are bad.

Most often, when we have successfully put on cultural celebration events, we may think that we have done a good job in teaching others to value diversity and we may conclude that things will get better. On the contrary; things may get worse before they get better, but that does not mean that people are taking a step backward in their development of cultural sensitivity. When we can no longer maintain the barriers of separation and have to deal with others who are different, we cannot help but react to it negatively. *Difference is bad.* This is an improvement from saying "difference does not exist," because at this level, they recognize that there are differences. However, we become very defensive and judgmental when we perceive the difference as a threat to us. Here we negatively evaluate and stereotype others and attribute undesirable characteristics to every member of that group. The ethnocentric response to difference in some ways is a natural reflex of our instinct to survive. It fuels the unholy fire of accusation, judgment, and mutual denigration with which we are already conditioned by society to obsess upon.

A woman named Mary, who worked in the International Students Services department of a major university, came to one of my intercultural workshops. At the recommendation of her supervisor, she came to find out why the international students were so "rude" to her in her office. I began the session with an exercise in which I asked the participants to imagine what society would be like if a certain cultural value was implicitly upheld by everyone. We were exploring the concept of a collectivistic society and I posed the question, "What would society be like if everyone implicitly believed that the goal of the group is more important than the goal of the individual?" While the rest of the group was quite comfortable with this exercise and was getting involved in sharing what this imaginary society would be like, Mary interrupted the group, saying, "But that's terrible. That's not right. Why should I give up my rights for the group? This would be like communism...." Every time a group member tried to explain to her that this was not necessarily bad, because many cultures of the world had this value, she just went on complaining how "un-American" these people are. At the end of the session, she insisted that I pray for her. "I am not a bad person," she assured me after we prayed. "I don't know why these international students are so rude to me." That was the last thing I remembered she said before she left. She never came back for the rest of the workshop.

4. It's okay for you to be different, but I am better.

Instead of putting down the differing others, a person with this kind of response will emphasize the positive and superior qualities of his/her cultural status. This ethnocentric response implies that the threatening cultural group is inferior and therefore makes one feel more secure. This shows up in the way the United States boasts about its technological superiority and the way we describe other countries as "underdeveloped." In 1990, every graduation speech that I heard at the University of Southern California mentioned what was happening in Eastern Europe, where people from Communist countries were demanding democracy from their governments. Whenever the speakers mentioned the subject, the audience would cheer. I could almost hear the audience saying, "We had it right all along." The assumption is that the people in these countries wanted to become like us. Here, difference is recognized—except *our* way of doing things is better. When this defense strategy is challenged, the most common response is, "So, what's wrong with being an American?"

My church, the Episcopal Church, has its roots in the Church of England. At no time would we denigrate others' ways of being Christian, but we certainly have much pride about being Anglican. We take pride in our democratic process in making church decisions. We are more than ready to show others how every time the Episcopal Church debates a controversial issue, "the world" is watching us. Affirmation of our strength is good and fine, but when we use our pride to assume superiority, implying that the differing others are inferior, we turn our pride into a golden calf. As a result, we climb higher in our ethnocentric tower and avoid interaction with people whom we imply to be lower.

5. I am different; therefore I am bad and you are good.

This ethnocentric response is the reversal of the previous two responses. People in this state denigrate themselves and their own culture in order to try to fit into the mainstream culture. They assume the dominant cultural group's attitude and sense of superiority by putting down their own cultural values, beliefs, customs, and community. For example, an American-born girl of Mexican descent came home from the first day of school and asked her parents, "Why is there something wrong with me? Why don't I have blonde hair and light skin like the other kids?"

I was in this state all through my teenage years in the United States. Everything from my Chinese culture was bad and counted as useless—language, customs, and family. Everything "American" was good—English, individualism, and competitiveness. The reason for me to choose this defense against difference was simple: it worked. It worked in getting me through college and into a good job. Being members of "minority" groups in this country forces us to go either back to being in denial—into our separated and isolated communities—or to go into reversal in order to survive. The win/lose mentality—the unholy fire—is so deep-seated in everything that we see and feel in this society, that we want to choose the winning side at all costs, even including denying both ourselves and our heritage.

I was having a conversation with the director of El Centro Chicano, the Hispanic student services department of a university in Los Angeles. He said, "I have to help my students to understand that if they get through college here, they will be changed. In order to survive here, they have to learn the Anglo way of behaving. The sad thing is that they can no longer go back to their own communities and be fully accepted as they were. If they are not careful, they might lose their own identity altogether. The other sad thing is that no matter how hard they try, they will never be fully accepted by the Anglo community either." The system of the dominant culture pushes members of the minority cultures into reversal; in other words, into assimilation. At the same time the same system would not fully accept those who have assimilated.

Many of the church's missionaries and Peace Corps volunteers, upon returning to the United States, have had a hard time readjusting because they were in this reversal stage. "Americans are so rude; I wish I were back in Africa," they lamented. Also, immigrants like me, who have spent a substantial amount of time in both their native culture and the mainstream American culture, are very often in this stage. I believe if the church nurtures people in this stage carefully to move on to the next stage, they can be a tremendous resource for multicultural ministry because their knowledge of the differing culture is much greater than those who have not gone through this stage of defense. I believe the church can do this by helping them to reaffirm their own culture while at the same time respecting their greater cross-cultural experience.

6. If you don't include like I do, you are bad.

As I gained more experience in working with people at various stages of the ethnocentric continuum, I discovered another form of defensive and judgmental responses which I found to be also ethnocentric—even though on the surface, it seems very inclusive. There is a whole generation of people who were raised to believe that one should not have any prejudices. In their formative years, they may have been reprimanded by their teachers or parents for using certain words or actions that were considered inappropriate and offensive. As a result, they learned not to be prejudiced in very specific behavioral ways that were not unlike a set of rules of conduct. They truly believed that if they followed these rules of inclusive conduct, they were free of prejudice. When they encountered others who did not behave the same way, they judged them as bad people. Even though this group of people believed that they were not prejudiced, their behavior and attitude toward someone who was different was a defensive and judgmental one. Their judgmental action was just as hurtful as a judgment coming from a historically dominant group against a minority group. They were defending their culture, which consisted of dos and don'ts regarding what it meant to be free of prejudice. In the midst of their trying to be good and inclusive people, they bought into the good/bad, right/wrong dichotomy. They hovered around the unholy fire, ready to point their fingers by judging others. Here was something that started out with very good intentions, but turned into a golden calf that we used to distance ourselves from others. We got back to our ethnocentric tower and climbed another level higher.

We tend to react to the last four kinds of judgmental responses toward difference by saying, "They're just misinformed." With that conclusion, we proceed to implement programs that give information about a particular group or culture, hoping that the information will correct this defensive attitude. The issue at this stage is not misinformation. The real issue is the lack of cultural knowledge of ourselves, and therefore true self-esteem. Our need to denigrate others who are different, thereby making ourselves superior, comes from the lack of in-depth knowledge of our cultural identity. With the person in reversal, the need to denigrate one's own culture in order to be accepted by the dominant culture is even a stronger indication of the lack of cultural self-esteem. If we are sure of our own cultural values and makeup, we would be less threatened by someone who acts differently and has different values and beliefs. Furthermore, we might even express an interest in finding out more about these differences, making the encounter into a learning experience. However, when we have not done our self-awareness and self-acceptance work, we would be more likely to be defensive in our initial reaction to someone who is different. In the win/lose mentality of our society, we don't have to do our internal work in order to gain an identity. The winner gains his or her identity from finding a loser. The judging one derives his or her identity as the superior one from the judged. By putting down others, we believe we are defending our identity.

> [Jesus said,] "Why do you see the speck in your neighbor's eye, but do not notice the log in your own eye? Or how can you say to your neighbor, 'Friend, let me take out the speck in your eye,' when you yourself do not see the log in your own eye? You hypocrite, first take the log out of your own eye, and then you will see clearly to take the speck out of your neighbor's eye."
>
> Luke 6:41–42

To counter the unholy fire of defensive denigration and judgment, we must invite, like Jesus did, people to look inward before they judge. "Take the log out of your own eye first." The issue here is the lack of cultural self-esteem. The most effective strategy is helping people to examine and affirm their own cultural values and beliefs. In a one-on-one dialogue, we can ask a person at this stage, "Before you talk about the others, let's talk about you. Tell me what's good about your culture, your upbringing, and your values."

Some might say, "But I don't have a culture. My family has been in the United States forever. I'm just an American." I would invite those who express this point of view to expand their perception of culture beyond race and ethnicity. Perhaps a more inclusive way to think about our culture is to explore our cultural "makeup," which encompasses the social, economic, spiritual, and psychological dimensions of our self-identity and worldviews. Some of us may incorporate a lot of our racial and ethnic identity in describing our cultural makeup, but that does not mean that everyone has to. For those of us who do not have an explicit ethnic identity, it is imperative that we explore our internal environment, which may include many unconscious values, beliefs, and assumptions. Only by increasing our self-awareness, which is a precursor to self-acceptance, can we build a stronger cultural self-esteem. When one is able to affirm one's cultural makeup, we can then continue our one-on-one dialogue; we can then ask, "Now that you know why your cultural values are good, can you imagine why the others' values and behaviors, even though they're different from yours, are good for them?"

Other effective strategies are intragroup dialogue and intergroup dialogue. Intragroup dialogue brings together people of similar cultural backgrounds to share and explore what it means to be a member of that group. In many Christian denominations, there are "racial–ethnic" ministry groups set up for this purpose. Many minority groups in the church and in the secular society have learned the importance of intragroup dialogue, through which they found mutual support and understanding while gaining a stronger group identity. The growing edge of this kind of program involves not only the minority groups, but the majority also. The Episcopal Church, in cooperation with the National Conference (formerly the National Conference of Christians and Jews) in Los Angeles in 1995, designed and implemented a "White Racial Awareness Program" in which "white" participants facilitated by "white" leaders explored what it meant to be "White Americans." As a result of this program, participants are more prepared to enter into intergroup dialogue after having gained a fuller, more secure self-identity. With the acceptance of our self-identity, we are less likely to judge others with whom we engage in intergroup dialogue. After taking the logs out of our own eyes, we see more clearly and are more ready to discuss objectively the speck in our neighbor's eye.

Intergroup dialogue brings together people from two or more cultural groups to explore in a constructive manner how they are different. An example of this kind of program is the "Interracial Dialogue Program" that I designed for the Diocese of Los Angeles after the 1992 riots. This dialogue program brought together churches of different cultural backgrounds and formed groups of fifteen to twenty-five individuals. They met five different times over a period of two months for constructive dialogue. With the help of skilled facilitators, participants learned more about their own cultures as well as those of others. I have included a modified version of the Interracial Dialogue Program in Appendix B.

7. I know there are differences, but they are not important.

People with this ethnocentric response emphasize the commonalities and downplay the differences among groups. While people at this stage are genuine in their desire to get along with others by finding similarities between their culture and the others, they nevertheless are still attempting to preserve the centrality of their own worldview. The issue here is that if I want to accept only the part of you that is like me, I am ignoring the rest of you that is different and I am not treating you as a whole person. In other words, I want to see only the part of you that affirms my identity. This attitude is the hardest to address because we cannot really argue with someone who says, "We are all human beings; deep down we are really all the same."

I have been to many meetings where a very fruitful discussion on differences was taking place. Inevitably, a well-meaning person would bring the discussion to a screeching halt by saying something like, "Why are we all wasting time talking about what divides us? We should be doing things that are common to all of us. We are all God's children. We are all equal before God and we should be doing God's work as one family." Of course everyone would agree, and we would bury once again an opportunity to learn about cultural difference.

In the early years of my work in multicultural ministry, I facilitated a multicultural young adult ministry conference. Much of the first half of the conference was devoted to creating a safe environment in which people could feel free to share their perspective of interracial and intercultural relations. Finally, a participant found enough courage to tell the group what it was like growing up as an African American in the United States. Before he finished, a European-American woman chimed in — "This is no different from my own experience growing up as a woman in a male-dominated society." Then she continued on with a litany of her own experiences of oppression.

"But it's not the same!" A person of color spoke out. Immediately the group was divided into two camps. The more the persons of color tried to say that there were differences, the more the European Americans disagreed.

"What you experienced was part of what all human beings have to get through growing up; black, white, Asian, or Hispanic.

There is no difference," the European Americans insisted. This argument continued for a few rounds and eventually the people of color got totally frustrated and stopped participating. They knew that recognizing cultural differences was very important for them to maintain their identities, but when differences were being trivialized, they interpreted that all this talk about oneness of humanity really meant everybody should become like European Americans. Trying to find commonalities is a genuine goodwill gesture in our wish to move toward a more harmonious multicultural community, but when finding commonalities becomes a device to trivialize others' values and beliefs, the result is just as damaging as the flat-out judgment of others of the earlier ethnocentric responses.

I was having a casual conversation with an Episcopal priest who was a member of the Commission on Ministry. One of the functions of the Commission on Ministry was to screen potential candidates who were seeking ordination in the church. I was working on my first book at the time, so naturally I started talking about the issues of raising up leadership in ethnic congregations. I talked about how people of color in the United States were culturally very different from European Americans and should be given special care and attention. For example, the traditional screening process, which required the candidate to boast voluntarily about his or her worthiness, was directly opposed to many of the Asian cultural values. Many Asian leaders were taught to be humble and not to stand out in the community. Therefore, perhaps, the Commission on Ministry should think about an alternative way of raising up leadership in ethnic congregations by "inviting" and nurturing potential candidates, rather than the traditional voluntary system. I thought I was making perfect sense until he interrupted me saying, "I have a lot of problems with what you are saying. Why should we give special treatment to ethnic candidates? We all had to go through the same process in order to be ordained. If they want to be ordained, they should go through the same thing that you and I went through. We can't have a double standard."

"We are all God's children." "We should be doing what is common to all of us." "We should not have a double standard." "We are all human beings, aren't we?" "There is only one God who is the Creator of all." These are the most common responses to cultural differences in a church discussion on multicultural issues. Granted, this kind of statement is an important piece of our faith which makes us the evangelistic religion that we are. Jesus came to save not just the Jews or the people around

Judea, but all peoples and all nations. However, more often than not, these statements are said as a way of trivializing differences that exist among cultures. I believe this minimizing response to difference is the biggest hurdle for the church to jump if we are to become a truly multicultural church.

The cause of this attitude may have something to do with the way we are raised. We were taught to find common ground. When we meet someone new, we tend to find something we have in common in order to establish a relationship. When this is taught over and over again, we may learn implicitly that we are not supposed to deal with differences. Perhaps we have also seen too many destructive behaviors as a result of dealing with differences. In our long history of "riots" or uprisings, racial discrimination, and mutually accusatory approaches in dealing with differences, we may have learned to avoid dealing with differences because we have implicitly learned that dealing with differences could result in conflict and destruction.

If the issue is the implicit belief that dealing with differences would be destructive, then to increase sensitivity we would need to learn that knowing differences can be and will be constructive and beneficial. An effective strategy is to provide experiential learning that supports why it is beneficial to know these differences. Examples of these kinds of learning activities would be role-playing, experiential exercises, and presentations that point out the kinds of trouble we could get into if we do not know about cultural differences. These kinds of programs should provide us with solutions and skills which, if practiced with the knowledge of cultural differences, can make us become better persons, better Christians, better leaders, and better ministers. In practical terms, this is the state when we can educate people with reports of cross-cultural experiences, bringing in people from other cultures to act as resources, and with illustrations of how cultural differences affect our interpretation of behavior. This process is most effective when we use experiential exercises that reveal the practical benefit of understanding differences for multicultural living. This kind of program will move people into a new paradigm in which they will no longer perceive their own cultural values and beliefs as absolutes and universal. They begin to notice that cultures are relative to each other. Bennett called this "ethnorelativism." This paradigm shift may cause disorientation and confusion at first. But if we take care in supporting them by acknowledging that these reactions are "normal," people will be more willing to stay in the process to move toward ethnorelativism.

[Jesus said,] "You have heard that it was said, 'You shall love your neighbor and hate your enemy.' But I say to you, Love your enemies and pray for those who persecute you, so that you may be children of your Father in heaven; for he makes his sun rise on the evil and on the good, and sends rain on the righteous and on the unrighteous. For if you love those who love you, what reward do you have? Do not even the tax collectors do the same? And if you greet only your brothers and sisters, what more are you doing that others? Do not even the Gentiles do the same? Be perfect, therefore, as your heavenly Father is perfect."

Matthew 5:43–48

In our towers of ethnocentricism, we put God within our cultural frame. We may be unable to distinguish the difference between our culture and God's culture. We believe that God is on our side and therefore, we can judge those who are not like us as the enemies. Ethnocentricism ultimately limits our perception of God. Jesus' challenge for us to love our enemies is an invitation to enter the new paradigm of ethnorelativism. Jesus wants us to be compassionate to our enemies understanding their perspectives and praying for them. For God does not favor one culture over another. God "makes his sun rise on the evil and on the good, and sends rain on the righteous and on the unrighteous." Even though most of us came to be in relationship with God within our own cultural boundaries, Jesus invites us to percieve God as outside our cultural frame of reference. When we do that, we can see God also interacting, challenging, and affirming other cultures that are different from ours. In the context of God's inclusiveness of all people, cultures are simply relative to each other. We cease to judge each other but accept each other as also being children of God. To be "perfect" in the context of the passage does not mean to be flawless. It means to be inclusive as God is inclusive; be compassionate as God is compassionate; be ethnorelative as God is ethnorelative.

In this chapter we have explored the steps we need to take in order to climb down from our towers of ethnocentrism moving toward the level ground of ethnorelativism. As we climb down from our towers, we examine our ethnocentric responses; we explore how we avoid dealing with differences with our golden calves, and why we judge others sitting around the unholy fire. As we climb down from our towers, we realize that God is not confined by the narrow dimensions of our ethnocentric towers. As we climb down from our towers, we recognize that we are not

God and therefore do not have the right to judge others as good or bad, right or wrong. As we climb down from our towers, we see God on the ground challenging and interacting with not just our people, but with all people independent of their cultural backgrounds. When we land on the ground, we face each other without negative preconceptions, but rather with acceptance. We speak honestly without blaming or judging others. We listen to each other as if the other is a prophetic voice calling us back to a clearer and more faithful vision of God. On the ground, we face our uncertainties with our faith in God. We build a holy fire around which we can share our stories about the pain of separation and the joy of reconciliation. We gather around the burning bush for communion.

CHAPTER EIGHT

Tending the Burning Bush on Level Ground: Maintaining Ethnorelativism

When we finally land on the level ground of ethnorelativism, where cultural differences are neither good nor bad, but only different, how do we maintain this openness? Tending the burning bush on level ground means maintaining ethnorelativism with the focus and help of God as our judge and comforter. Ethnorelativism is not a natural human inclination. Ethnorelativism may cause us to feel disoriented and insecure when we feel there is no solid ground to stand on. How do we make decisions when all cultural values are relative? Does that mean that anything goes? The uncertainties that we face are constant challenges to our need for security and order. The temptation to come up with a new set of rules, creating a golden calf that we can simply follow, is too great. How do we keep the burning bush going on level ground when the temptation to make things static and to build another tower of Babel is so great? In order to learn to maintain ethnorelativism in our multicultural community, we again need to explore what it is like being ethnorelative. How do we know that we are being ethnorelative? With this understanding, then we can explore how we can foster and maintain such an multicultural community. I will present five different ethnorelative responses to difference. They follow fairly closely the ethnorelative stages of Bennett's theory. Again they are arranged progressively according to the intercultural sensitivity developmental process.[1]

1. Willingness to live in the uncertainty of being nonjudgmental.

> The scribes and the Pharisees brought a woman who had been caught in adultery; and making her stand before all of them, they said to him [Jesus], "Teacher, this woman was caught in the very act of committing adultery. Now in the law Moses commanded us to stone such women. Now what do you say?" They said this to test him, so that they might have some charge to bring against him. Jesus bent down and wrote with his finger on the ground. When they kept on questioning him, he straightened up and said to them, "Let anyone among you who is without sin be the first to throw a stone at her." And once again he bent down and wrote on the ground. When they heard it, they went away, one by one, beginning with the elders; and Jesus was left alone with the woman standing before him.
>
> John 8:3–9

The crowd, led by the scribes and the Pharisees, judged this woman as a sinner. They wanted to apply Moses' law strictly according to the letter. She was caught sinning; she had to be stoned. The law for them was a static thing, a ruler by which they measured and judged each person without regard for the context—a golden calf. Jesus turned the whole situation around by asking them to look inward instead of outward. By looking inward, they moved from perceiving themselves as the righteous ones to realizing that they were sinners too. By looking at their own sin, they began to see that their sinfulness was only relative

---

[1] Bennett's theory consists of three ethnorelative states: Acceptance, Adaptation, and Integration. Each state is further divided into two stages. The first response I describe here corresponds to the Acceptance state. The second and third responses correspond to the Empathy and Pluralism stages of Adaptation. The fourth and fifth responses correspond to the Contextual Evaluation and Constructive Marginality stages of Integration. See Milton J. Bennett, "A Developmental Approach to Training for Intercultural Sensitivity," in *Theories and Methods in Cross-Cultural Orientation,* ed. Judith N, Martin, International Journal of Intercultural Relations, Vol. 5, No. 2 (New York/Oxford/Beijing/Frankfurt/Sao Paulo/Sydney/Tokyo/Toronto: Pergamon Press, 1986), pp.179–196 and Milton J. Bennett, "Towards Ethnorelativism: A Developmental Model of Intercultural Sensitivity," in *Cross-Cultural Orientation,* ed. R. Michael Paige (Lanham, Maryland: University Press of America, 1986), pp. 46–69.

to this woman's sin. Jesus' challenging question put all of them on the same level ground. They were forced to come down from their towers and regard the woman not as inferior to them but as an equal. By looking inward, the crowd stopped judging and dispersed.

When we judge, we treat cultural values and assumptions as static things. With this static perception of values, we proceed to use our values as a ruler to measure others as good or bad, right or wrong. In order not to judge others so readily, we must learn that a value is not a thing but a process. In the process of valuing, we have to take our cultural contexts into consideration, because depending on each unique cultural context, the values at which this process arrives can change depending on the time and place in which the process takes place.[2] When values are taught without the valuing process, that value can become a static thing—an ethnocentric absolute that we use to judge ourselves and others. For example, in the movement to change our language to make it more inclusive, we tried to use alternative words to replace those that were considered sexist. Why? We changed those words because the sexist words were part of an oppressive system that continuously and unconsciously put women at a disadvantage. By changing the language, we were hoping to make an impact and thereby to change this sexist system. However, in the process of propagating this change, we forgot to emphasize the reason why we wanted these changes. As a result, a whole generation knew only that there was a set of words that we were not supposed to use anymore. Without learning the valuing process of why we wanted the change, all they knew was that it was wrong. We gave it a label called "politically correct," and used it to judge others who still used those words.

In order to stop ourselves from judging, we must create an environment that encourages the inward reflection through which we can ensure that our value remains a process relative to our cultural context. When we find ourselves wanting to judge someone or a group, we must first look inward and find out what values or beliefs within us are being threatened. Then we must recapture the process of how we gain these values and beliefs. Only after that can we let go of our cultural values as a static thing we use to judge others and allow our values to continue to

---

[2]See Milton J. Bennett, "Towards Ethnorelativism: A Developmental Model of Intercultural Sensitivity," in *Cross-Cultural Orientation,* ed. R. Michael Paige (Lanham, Maryland: University Press of America, 1986), pp. 49–50.

be a process that evolves and changes according to the context we are in.

After we look inward and stop ourselves from judging, we are then more ready to accept others who behave differently. Furthermore, we also become very curious about the valuing process behind the others' behavior. "Why is this different way of doing things important to them?" For example, if after a meal, a person across the table belches loudly, an ethnocentric response may be "That's so rude!" (difference is bad), or "It doesn't matter, it's just a human biological reaction" (difference is not important). A person with an nonjudgmental attitude will not minimize the difference or put it down, but react with interest. "Isn't that an interesting behavior? I wonder what the value behind it is." The person may proceed to investigate by asking questions and may even discover that belching in some cultures may mean that the food is excellent. When we achieve the non-judgmental ability, we are open to a whole world of exciting learning when we encounter people of different cultural backgrounds. The differing others are no longer a threat to us, but rather represent an opportunity for inward reflection and discovery and outward appreciation and learning about other cultures and the valuing process.

I was visiting a senior pastor who was charged by the bishop to start a Commission on Asian Ministry. He was worrying about how he, as a European American, could run the first meeting of the commission effectively. The members of the commission included Japanese, Chinese, Koreans and Filipinos. He observed in the past that some of the commission members were very quiet and verbally did not participate much. He also observed that there were a couple of Asian pastors who acted very authoritatively and sometimes fought with each other. He asked with great curiosity, "Can you tell me something about their cultures that explains why they behaved that way? How would they behave when I am the authoritative figure? I know my style of leadership would definitely not work with this group." I started talking about how different cultures understand power and authority differently.[3] Some members of the group would treat him as an authority figure and would defer to him for any decision that needed to be made. They would expect to be invited to speak. That was why they were quiet. However, some of the Asian church leaders, who had been in leadership positions for a long time, would expect to have authority at all times. As I was

---

[3]See Eric H. F. Law, *The Wolf Shall Dwell with the Lamb* (St. Louis: Chalice Press, 1993), pp. 13–28.

describing these cultural differences, a part of me was worried that I might have started an unholy fire. He might respond ethnocentrically, like the priest I mentioned in the last chapter. But his reaction was one of amazement and interest. "So what can I do?" he asked. I was relieved.

I suggested that he consider using an introduction exercise called "reporters." Instead of initiating a discussion by asking people to volunteer their thoughts and ideas, this dialogue process invited group members to find a partner and form a pair. In each pair, they would take turns playing reporter by asking a few questions and then recording their partner's answers. When they had finished interviewing each other, each person reported back to the group what his or her partner had said. This exercise was designed with sensitivity to the different perceptions of power. It allowed those who did not believe they had power, to speak up and be listened to by one other person. It also allowed those who believed they should have authority the respect they needed as they were being interviewed. As I described this process, I could see his eyes light up. At the end, he thanked me and said that for the first time he understood the values and reasons why many of the Asians whom he encountered behaved the way they did. A week later, he called me to let me know that the exercise worked very well.

Not everyone will be as open and ready to accept the different behaviors and values as was the pastor mentioned above. In order to maintain a multicultural community, we must foster an environment where people can continuously maintain this open acceptance of behavior without judgment. Furthermore, we must also constantly teach each other to recapture the valuing process. This is what the intragroup and intergroup dialogue processes can do. In a dialogue process, we help participants to regain and understand their own valuing process while they learn about others. In a dialogue process, participants are often surprised by how two people who share the same values can have such a different process of arriving at the same values. By understanding this difference in the valuing process, we learn to value each other's cultural context, which is an integral part of the process as well. In chapter ten we will discuss how, through the dialogue process, we can help a community sustain this accepting attitude by using the technique of setting ground rules for dialogue.

2. Learning to be "interpathic" to others who are different.

David Augsburger, in his book *Cross-Cultural Counseling,* makes the distinction among the terms *sympathy, empathy,* and *interpathy.*[4] I am sympathetic when I react spontaneously to your feelings based on my frame of reference. Usually I draw from my experience of a similar event in order to sympathize with you. In sympathy, I may project my own inner feelings upon you, assuming that your process and experience is the same as mine. In other words, sympathy can be interpreted as an ethnocentric way of "feeling with" others.

When I am empathetic to you, I recognize your feelings as separate from mine but I still draw from my own experience, my own frame of reference, in my response to you. I rely and search for common cultural assumptions, values, and patterns of thinking from which to understand and respond to your feelings. In empathy, my experience is the frame; your pain is the picture. Empathy as defined by Augsburger may still be an ethnocentric response in that it may minimize cultural differences.

Augsburger invented a third word to describe a ethnorelative way of "feeling with" others—interpathy. When I am interpathic to you, I temporarily step out of my frame of reference and enter into yours so that I can fully understand your feeling as you understand it yourself. Interpathy does not require that we share a set of common experiences, values, and assumptions. I accept and embrace what is truly yours. Your experiences becomes both frame and picture.

Matthew Fox called this compassion. "Compassion is not knowing about the suffering and pain of others. It is, in some way, knowing that pain, entering into it, sharing it and tasting it insofar as that is possible....But how does one know another's feeling and not merely know about it? Imagination is absolutely necessary for such a compassionate learning experience."[5]

When I gave a workshop on understanding Asian Pacific Americans, one of the resources I used was short summaries of the history of the various Asian and Pacific Islander groups in the United States.[6] I invited the participants to pick an Asian-Pacific group and to imagine how they would feel and what value they would hold if they had the same history. The next step was for

---

[4] See David W. Augsburger, *Pastoral Counseling Across Cultures* (Philadelphia: The Westminster Press, 1986), pp.17–47.

[5] Matthew Fox, *A Spirituality Names Compassion and the Healing of the Global Village, Humpty Dumpty and Us* (Minneapolis: Winston Press, 1979), p. 21.

[6] A good source for Asian Pacific immigration history up to 1980 is Tricia Knoll, *Becoming Americans—Asian Sojourners, Immigrants, and Refugees in the Western United States* (Portland, Oregon: Coast to Coast Books, 1980), pp. 13–28.

them to explore how the different Asian-Pacific groups would organize their lives in the United States with these derived values. Since this particular group I was working with had experienced much intercultural sensitivity training, they were able to leave their own cultural frame of reference temporarily and participate in this process of creative imagination. At the end of the session, the participants got in touch with the pain and discrimination experienced by the different Asian-Pacific groups in America— Chinese, Japanese, Korean, Vietnamese, and Filipino. As a result, they began to understand why many of the Asian Americans they worked with did not trust the institution, and therefore did not participate in the democratic process in church and in American society. The understanding derived from this creative imagination process was not a shallow assumption of commonness characterized by the ethnocentric response that minimizes differences. Interpathy can only happen when we enable people to let go of their own frame of reference and enter into another worldview so that they can experience and know how others feel.

Providing experiential activity in which one cultural group can interpathically understand another cultural group is essential in maintaining the burning bush of a multicultural community. Besides the process of imagination, we can also provide opportunities for people from different cultural backgrounds to express their innermost feelings and beliefs while enabling others to listen without the screen of their own cultural frame. Many dialogue processes such as "A Time When I Felt Different"[7] and "Photolanguage"[8] increase the likelihood that interpathy can take place when persons of different cultural backgrounds encounter each other.

3. Commitment to cultural pluralism.

A multicultural community must foster the commitment to accept and work through the existence of more than one cultural framework within the community. We must continuously affirm that not only are there culture differences, but that these differences must always be understood totally within the context of the relevant culture. We can arrive at such a commitment only after repeatedly providing actual experiences of interpathy in which one cultural group can truly experience and see and feel the other's perspective. A community with this commitment will not

---

[7]See Session One of Appendix B.
[8]See Eric H. F. Law, *The Wolf Shall Dwell with the Lamb* (St. Louis: Chalice Press, 1993), pp. 115–120.

act or decide until the issue at hand is truly understood within the context of each different cultural framework.

While I was doing research for this book in Hawaii, I interviewed a number of church leaders who were known to be respected intercultural leaders. Many of these leaders had worked for a long period of time in an ethnic community other than their own. One of the characteristics that they demonstrated was that they would not make a decision until they could understand the situation from the different cultural worldviews of the community. They spent much time listening, observing, and processing information whenever they were in an uncertain situation. Their absolute commitment to cultural pluralism was what gained them respect from the different ethnic communities.

A pastor of Mexican-American background who worked in a bilingual congregation described his internal commitment to cultural pluralism and the concerns that came with it. He said, "Very often, it involved bringing half the congregation to understand the spirituality of the other half. So while I may understand both sides, I've got to, at any given moment, have my shoes on one side or the other. People will come and ask me if the hymns or the prayer book are better in English than in Spanish. And I really want to say, 'No, it just depends. Page so-and-so may be great in English, and the other page may be great in Spanish.' I feel I could easily float back and forth between them and I could enjoy them both. Yet I have to resonate with people who can enjoy only one half of it and make them feel that I value the one half that they can appreciate as much as the one half that the other side appreciates. And this is not always easy to do."

As I explored more deeply the concept of cultural pluralism, I realized that the Christian concept of the incarnation was God's commitment to cultural pluralism. The only difference was that in the case of Jesus, the two cultures were the divine and the human. The most distinctive element about Christianity was that God became human through Jesus in order to bring salvation to all people. Through Jesus, God committed to understand humankind only through the complete human frame of reference. Therefore, Jesus was born into the world through a woman as all humans are. Jesus experienced growing up, working as a carpenter, and struggling to realize his call to be the Messiah. Jesus experienced the joy and pain of friendship. Jesus experienced loving and being loved. Jesus faced rejection, betrayal, doubt, suffering, and finally death. Jesus' life was God's commitment to understand human beings on our terms. God, through Jesus, stepped out of the divine and entered into the human experience totally and completely. In the process, Jesus showed the world that a human being can be holy by his compassion for the poor, the oppressed, the powerless, the outcasts, and the "foreigners." In this sense, through exercising interpathy and commitment to cultural pluralism, we are responding to God's call for us to be holy. "Be compassionate, even as your Father is compassionate" (Luke 6:36, The Jerusalem Bible).

To maintain a multicultural community, we must continuously commit ourselves to cultural pluralism. We can invite the community to enter into a dialogue process in which each cultural group is empowered to communicate effectively their feelings and perspectives. We must also enable each cultural group to listen, digest, and reflect back to the whole community the different cultural perspectives that they have heard. Only after we have heard and understood these different perspectives can we appreciate the fuller, more complete portrait of the issues and concerns of the whole community. This process takes time and commitment from all in the community.

4. Learning to do contextual evaluation.

One might ask, "If everything is accepted and everything is relative, then how can we make any decisions?" When we climb down from our towers of ethnocentrism, we finally realize that our view of the world is not universal and that everything that is different should not be judged, but deserves to be explored and understood. But with this attitude, are we not facing the danger of being so open-minded that we may be incapable of making decisions regarding what is right or wrong? While we must validate the need to suspend judgment in order to climb down from our tower of ethnocentrism and to develop our interpathy skills and commitment to cultural pluralism, we must also advance our ability to make evaluative decisions as individuals and as a community.

The ability to make moral and ethical decisions based on contextual evaluation is the key to further development of a multicultural community. Contextual evaluation is the ability to analyze and evaluate situations relative to different cultural contexts. The end result of contextual evaluation is a judgment based on the relative goodness of the different cultural values involved but conditioned by the situation in which the judgment has to be made. This is similar to the concept of power analysis[9]

---

[9]See Eric H. F. Law, *The Wolf Shall Dwell with the Lamb* (St. Louis: Chalice Press, 1993), pp. 53–62.

I put forth in my previous book, *The Wolf Shall Dwell with the Lamb*. For example, I was working with a group composed of half English-speakers and half bilingual Spanish/English-speakers. After an initial round of mutual invitation, where we introduced and shared some information about ourselves to each other, I realized the varying English-language skills of the bilingual participants; some were speaking very briefly and were often embarrassed about the way they used the language. I did a quick contextual evaluation and decided to divide the group into an English-speaking group and a Spanish-speaking group. I gave them two questions to discuss and invited someone from each group to record a summary of what group members said on a large piece of paper. After they returned to the large group and reported to each other in both languages, one person complained, "Why were we separated? The whole purpose of your working with us was to help us integrate with each other. I didn't like being separated from the other group."

At that point, I realized that I had done a contextual evaluation but did not inform the group how I did it. So I explained, "I understand that there is a very strong value behind keeping the group together." I was speaking to the English-speaking participants. "I too believe that integration is good. On the other hand, based on my assessment of our initial sharing, I realized that some members, whose primary language was not English, would probably prefer to speak Spanish in order to express themselves better."

"We can translate what everybody said and not be separated," replied the speaker who initally voiced his concern.

"Yes," I said, "the logical conclusion would be to run the meeting bilingually in which everything is translated into both languages. But we have only one and one-half hours for the meeting, and if everything was translated, we would not be able to get through our agenda. This was the reason I divided you into two groups. I knew it was uncomfortable for some of you. But look at the end result. The reports from both groups were very honest and in-depth because in the smaller group each person can speak comfortably and with more time. If we had to stay in the large group all of this time, we would not have time to finish our agenda and I can bet that the Spanish-speaking members would not have communicated as much in this meeting."

At that point, a few of the Spanish-speakers concurred with me. With this explanation, the group was satisfied. In this situation, I put to use contextual evaluation by first evaluating how the English-speakers judged the situation and then I evaluated how the Spanish-speakers judged the situation. Then I added my evaluation based on the context of the meeting, especially regarding the time limit. Putting all the evaluations together, I made a judgment based on the relative goodness of each perspective, and chose to segregate the group temporarily, knowing that this would be contrary to a deeply held value of the English-speaking group. Then I dealt with the consequences of my decision seriously by explaining the greater value of honest communication as the basis of my action.

Contextual evaluation has to be part of the skills that a multicultural community must develop. If we do not develop this ability, we would become a community that is paralyzed with indecision. We would spend all of our time trying to maintain ourselves, learning only to get along with each other and never to move out into the world to do the work of justice.

As Christians, we have another context to consider in our work of contextual evaluation, in addition to our different cultural contexts. We have to take God's context into account. After we explore the different cultural perspectives, we have to ask, "What would God say in this situation? How does the gospel inform us in our decision making process?" God becomes the judge of the relative goodness of our cultural values. With God as our judge and nurturer, we can decide what is right not according to our own cultural context, but according to God's. By doing contextual evaluation with God in the picture, we are truly tending the burning bush that empowers us to stand up in the world and do the work of justice.

To foster and nurture this ability to do contextual evaluation, we can provide opportunities to do theological reflection, especially through studying scriptures together in a multicultural context. In our dialogue with each other and with scripture, we explore scripture from its own historical context and then we explore how it interfaces with our different cultural contexts. As each cultural group shares its perspective, we begin to see how God can be seen apart from our own cultures. We begin to see the vision of God more clearly. We begin to see our call to ministry more decisively.

5. Living the spirituality of creative marginality.

If we practice interpathy, cultural pluralism, and contextual evaluation regularly for a long period of time, we may feel marginalized if we do not have the support of a multicultural community. When differences are constantly integrated into one's worldview, we feel that we can no longer identify ourselves as a member of any specific culture. We face the danger of not belonging to any one specific cultural group.

A bilingual pastor described himself as being in the "third camp." He once said, "As a bicultural and bilingual person, I'm never fully part of one or the other language group. I can fully feel the enmity that one camp may have for the other. Even when I'm really mad, let's say, at the Hispanics, I always have one foot in that camp. And when I'm really mad at the Anglos, there's always a part of me that still understands them. It's hard to be 100 percent in one camp or another. In fact, I would say it's impossible."

Frequently in an intercultural sensitivity-training workshop, after I have described the ethnocentric and ethnorelative stages, a few people would come up and thank me personally for telling them that it was "normal" for someone to feel marginalized and to not fit into any cultural group. They also thanked me for pointing out that they had a unique gift that could be used constructively to mediate between cultural groups. These persons usually grew up in a multi-cultural household or had spent a major part of their lives immersed in another culture. In these cases, I always saw a total change of attitude and outlook—from being withdrawn and disconnected, to having more self-confidence and getting involved. The multicultural community needs to appreciate and even seek out these marginalized people, because of their unique gift—living between cultures. If they are given the appropriate support and training, they can become a major force in enabling the church to move toward being a multicultural, ethnorelative church.

In the Judeo-Christian tradition, there is something to be said about the spirituality of the marginalized—people who don't belong. Many of the important figures in the Scriptures were in some way marginalized people. Abraham and Sarah and the generations after them up to Joseph were sojourners. Moses started out in Egypt and in his adult life, found himself between the enslaved Israelites and Pharaoh. Look what he did in negotiating with Pharaoh and liberating the Israelites. St. Paul was a devout Jew who persecuted Christians, but later discovered Christianity himself. Look what he was able to accomplish in bringing the gospel to the Gentile nations. Jesus was very often in the company of the marginal people. In another way, Jesus was marginal in that he was living between the realms of the divine and the human.

The creativity that can happen when people are in between is remarkable. It often shows in the courage and the faith they have in God. It is like a string on a musical instrument, which is nothing more than a wire connecting two points. If there is no tension, there is no sound. If there is too much tension, the string will break. If the string is tightened with the right amount of tension, it makes a beautiful sound. Culturally marginal people, if nurtured, can be the bridge between cultures. If they are pushed too hard to choose one culture over another, they will snap and lose connection with both groups. If they are not nurtured, they can be perceived as lost people wandering from place to place, looking for the right community in which to belong. The Christian church has the great potential to affirm these people, because our tradition is full of marginal people who had a great deal to contribute to the livelihood of the church. A multicultural community will produce people who live the spirituality of creative marginality. They are a people whom we have sent out into the world to mediate differences and conflicts among groups. They are nomads, sojourners; ever wandering on the ground, challenging the ethnocentric towers, calling forth people to come down. They are a people we must support, nurture, and empower to be our guides as we engage in dialogue with each other on level ground. They are the tenders of the burning bush.

CHAPTER NINE

Today I Set Before You Life and Death...Choose Life!

If you obey the commandments of the LORD your God that I am commanding you today, by loving the LORD your God, walking in his ways, and observing his commandments, decrees, and ordinances, then you shall live and become numerous, and the LORD your God will bless you in the land that you are entering to possess. But if your heart turns away and you do not hear, but are led astray to bow down to other gods and serve them, I declare to you today that you shall perish; you shall not live long in the land that you are crossing the Jordan to enter and possess. I call heaven and earth to witness against you today that I have set before you life and death, blessings and curses. Choose life so that you and your descendants may live, loving the LORD your God, obeying him, and holding fast to him...

Deuteronomy 30:16–20a

So far we have had discussion in some detail about how we are prone to choose death by bowing down to other gods. We choose death by building our towers of ethnocentrism, obsessing over the unholy fire of judging others, and creating the golden calf to avoid dealing with the uncertainty created by intercultural encounters. We have explored how we can begin to choose life by creating opportunities for intercultural encounters through intragroup and intergroup dialogue, and through experiential learning, in which we learn to be nonjudgmental, increase our interpathic skills, commit ourselves to cultural pluralism, exercise contextual evaluation, and live in the spirituality of marginality.

But choosing life is not a one-time deal. Neither is it a linear process. After we have worked so hard coming down from our towers and maintaining the fire on level ground, we may assume that we will stay ethnorelative the rest of our lives. The temptation is to take a snapshot of the burning bush, put it on a pedestal, and treat it as a god, making it into a golden calf. We may observe God's commandments, decrees, and ordinances, but can we continue to love God and walk in God's way keeping our covenant with God a dynamic living process? The temptation to fall back into choosing death is so great that we cannot afford to stop working toward ethnorelativism again and again.

> Six days later, Jesus took with him Peter and James and his brother John and led them up a high mountain, by themselves. And he was transfigured before them, and his face shone like the sun, and his clothes became dazzling white. Suddenly there appeared to them Moses and Elijah," talking with him. Then Peter said to Jesus, "Lord, it is good for us to be here; if you wish, I will make three dwellings here, one for you, one for Moses and one for Elijah." While he was still speaking, suddenly a bright cloud overshadowed them, and from the cloud a voice said, "This is my Son, the Beloved; with him I am well pleased; listen to him!" When the disciples heard this, they fell to the ground and were overcome by fear. But Jesus came and touched them, saying "Get up and do not be afraid." And when they looked up, they saw no one except Jesus himself alone.
>
> Matthew 17:1–8

Peter had a relationship with Jesus that had taught him much about relating to God as a dynamic process, not just as a straight adherence to the law. But at the sight of the Transfiguration, where he finally understood how Jesus related to the law and the prophets—Moses and Elijah—he allowed his human instinct to want things to become static to take over. "I will build three dwellings here," he declared. What for? So that Peter and the others could sit there all day and all night on the mountaintop, thereby ignoring the real ministries they were called to do? Peter tried to turn the process of understanding Jesus in the context of the law and the prophets into a static thing that he could sit and adore. Peter tried to turn this vision, this understanding, into the golden calf. Choosing life is a decisive process that we must practice all the time. We have to keep this process conscious at all times, or we will end up unknowingly building a golden calf.

The trap of the golden-calf syndrome is there at every turn of our movement toward a multicultural community. Even when we think we have arrived at being a true ethnorelative community, we are still vulnerable to the attack of the golden calf. I was teaching a course on multicultural ministry. As part of the practical aspect of the course, I had invited leaders from the local church communities that had some success in building a multicultural community to share their insight and experience. One of the groups I invited was from a well-known multicultural church in the area. Many church leaders had used this church as a model and an ideal vision of what a multicultural congregation was like. As they presented their story of their church, a very apparent thing was surfacing. They spoke as if they had integrated the different cultural values within themselves. They even said that they didn't think of each other as specific ethnic persons. They were just people who were open-minded and accepting of each other. They then described their place of worship, which included displays of non-explicitly Christian artifacts from the cultures represented in their church. Then one of the students asked, "What happens when a newcomer arrives at your church and they can't deal with all of these artifacts in your church, and are frightened by the wide-openness of your thinking?"

"I guess they don't belong, then," replied one of the speakers, speaking in no uncertain terms.

After the presenters left, my students asked me with great concern, "How can that be an ideal model for a multicultural congregation? They are just as exclusive as a white church that turns every non-white person away."

Here was a group of people who had no doubt worked very hard to come down from their towers of ethnocentrism. They had moved beyond the acceptance of differences and arrived at a point where they were practicing the spirituality of creative marginality. But no sooner had they discovered this wonderful vision of a truly ethnorelative community than they built another tower that set them apart from others who had not made it to their level of sensitivity. They had forgotten the process by which they had gotten to where they were. The end product became the static ruler with which they measured others. They had created a golden calf. They got into the comfortableness of their vision up on the high mountain, and they wanted to build a permanent dwelling for this vision. But the minute we try to do that, we have chosen death. The moment we decide that we have the truth, we have laid the first brick of that new tower of Babel. The moment we think that we are better than others, we lay another brick on top of another brick. The moment we try to wrap up what we considered good into neat little packages, we have contributed another piece of our gold that will be molded into a golden calf.

Choosing life is not the same thing as a piece of paper that certifies us as nonprejudicial people who believe that all cultures are relative and that God is the ultimate judge. The choice between life and death is an ongoing process in which we utilize our hearts to commit to cultural pluralism, our minds to do contextual evaluation, and our bodies to act as agents for justice according to the gospel. When we stop using our hearts, minds, and bodies for this process, we have chosen death. God through Christ challenges us again and again not to reject the death of static absolutes, but to choose life by reentering the uncertainty of continual inclusivity. We must continue to struggle with welcoming people who are different—not just culturally, but also different in terms of their level of intercultural sensitivity.

If the church is to become a multicultural church, we must accept that people will be entering into this community at various stages of their intercultural sensitivity development. Some will be responding to differences ethnocentrically. Some will embrace differences with acceptance and curiosity. The real test of a true multicultural community is whether all these people can be accepted as part of the community. In other words, being ethnorelative cannot be a requirement to be part of a multicultural community. A multicultural community must not become static, but remain an open process. Entering a multicultural community is a journey, asking us to climb down from our ethnocentric towers as well as gathering us on level, ethnorelative ground. The role of the multicultural community is to provide a road map toward ethnorelativism. As people venture into this journey, the community affirms them at each stage of their expedition. The community also encourages and supports them to continue to move toward ethnorelativism at each crossing. One organization in which I witness this kind of community as a journey is Alcoholics Anonymous (AA).

The first time I went to an AA meeting, the sense of acceptance in the room was amazing to me. There were people at every step of the twelve-step program. Yet no one was put down because he or she was at an earlier stage of recovery. You could walk in stinking drunk and you would be welcome. How was this accomplished? First, there were enough people in the room who had gone through the recovery process and knew what it was like; therefore they could understand, empathize, and interpathize. Second, the twelve steps were read at every meeting. Even though many of the people had no idea of what it would be like at step five or six or twelve, they knew there was evidence in the room that said, "Stick with this, and you will see the light." There was a constant reassurance that people were on the right track by being there, even though people might be experiencing great disappointment and pain. Third, one slogan of AA is "one day at a time," expressing the need to struggle with the need to drink alcohol all the time. The greatest temptation for a recovering alcoholic is to start thinking that he or she is cured, and therefore no longer needs to attend any more AA meetings. This, from their experience, is a sure way to ruin their sobriety. Recovering from alcoholism is a lifelong process, and attending meetings regularly is a way to stay on track in the recovery process.

We have a lot to learn from an organization like AA if we are to develop a true multicultural community. In some ways, moving toward ethnorelativism is a journey with different milestones. The road map is the movement from ethnocentrism to ethnorelativism. One can enter the journey at any stage of intercultural sensitivity development. This community needs to present the commitment it will take in order for a person to enter this journey. We need to present what it is like to climb down from our towers of ethnocentrism with a fair amount of detail and realistic expectations at each step down. This community needs to include people who have gone through the journey at least once to be mentors to the ones at earlier stages. This community needs to reassure people that they are on the right track, especially when they are struggling with the disturbing need to judge others or the confusion that comes with finding meaning in the midst of relative cultural values and beliefs.

Like the AA process, our journey is not a one-time journey, but a recovery process. As we move down from our tower of ethnocentrism, there is always the temptation to move back up. We are constantly recovering from our tendency to react ethnocentrically to differences. We are constantly recovering from the need to create a golden calf. We are constantly recovering from committing adultery against God. Therefore, like the AA process, a multicultural community must gather regularly and consistently so that we can remind each other of our commitment and nurture each other in our journey.

The first task to developing a multicultural community is to develop the process that we will use regularly and consistently at our intercultural gatherings. I believe one of the processes that can serve this purpose is what I call the dialogue process. In chapters 10 and 11, I will describe in practical terms what the dialogue process is and how we can make it happen. Furthermore, in chapter 12, I will explore how the dialogue process can become like a liturgy that we can enact regularly in order to keep the burning bush present in the multicultural community. Finally, in chapter 13, I will discuss how our church liturgies can benefit from the dialogue process, making them more inclusive of different cultural groups.

CHAPTER TEN

Lighting, Sanctifying, and Maintaining the Holy Fire Through Dialogue

The intercultural dialogue process lights the fire by bring-ing together people from diverse ethnic and cultural backgrounds. When they gather, the dialogue process sanctifies the fire by providing a nonjudgmental environment in which they can discuss a common subject with the understanding that there will be different points of view and cultural perspectives. The primary purpose of dialogue is for each person to learn from the other so that he or she can change and grow. In the dialogue process, we provide activities to help participants practice being nonjudgmental, and to listen interpathically to each other. The dialogue process maintains the holy fire by holding up the value of cultural pluralism, developing the participants' skill in contextual evaluation, and moving them into constructive action to do justice. The dialogue process further affirms the spirituality of marginality as we wander in between cultures. The dialogue is the burning bush that draws us together to form a multicultural community where we can deal with intercultural issues without consuming each other. In this chapter we will focus on the practical. What do we do in order to develop this multicultural community? I have divided the dialogue process into three sections:

1. Lighting the Fire
2. Sanctifying the Fire
3. Maintaining the Holy Fire

These three components are not always separated when we implement them. Sometimes we combine all three into one activity; sometimes we focus on only one component with a number of activities. But for the purpose of clarity, I will discuss them separately and then address how and when to integrate them.

Lighting the Fire

When people are in isolation or self-imposed insulation, they deny that there are differences or they distance themselves from others who are different by avoiding any contact. Some of the frequently heard answers from many of the pre-dialogue surveys are:

- I don't need to attend any intercultural dialogue program because I don't have a problem with it.
- I don't need to deal with intercultural issues because there is none that I can see in our church.
- We are a very multicultural church and we get along fine.
- We are fine the way we are; we don't need anyone to come and create problems by talking about race and prejudice.

When we hear reactions like these, we have to find a way to light the fire so that they will not continue to avoid intercultural contacts. However, we cannot force them to engage in dialogue without any preparations, because they will only light an unholy fire with a lot of accusations and judgment. Lighting the fire means bringing people who are in denial together in a positive, nonthreatening environment in which differences are simply presented to them. They should be willing to come—if not for learning and dialogue, at least for curiosity's sake.

> When the day of Pentecost had come, they were all together in one place. And suddenly from heaven there came a sound like the rush of a violent wind, and it filled the entire house where they were sitting. Divided tongues, as of fire, appeared among them, and a tongue rested on each of them. All of them were filled with the Holy Spirit and began to speak in other languages, as the Spirit gave them ability. Now there were devout Jews from every nation under heaven living in Jerusalem. And at this sound the crowd gathered and was bewildered, because each one heard them speaking in the native language of each.

Amazed and astonished, they asked, "Are not all these who are speaking Galileans?"

Acts 2:1–7

Lighting a fire is equivalent to creating this "sound" that can be heard by people who might not readily participate in an intercultural dialogue event. But upon hearing this sound, they gather. When we hold such an event, we must speak the languages of the people and show them that there are differences among cultures and that knowing the differences is important. Many organizations invite me to come in to do interracial dialogue programs, yet after doing an initial assessment, I have often discovered that the majority of the people in an organization are not ready to engage in constructive dialogue. A typical recommendation is to plan a "noisy" event with very limited commitment. In this event, we do many nonthreatening activities that may include cultural sharing of food, customs, music, and dances. Along with these activities, we would do some minimal dialogue process that shows the participants that there are cultural differences not only on the surface but deep down in our internal cultures. (The Intercultural Dialogue/Worship Service described in Appendix A is an example of this kind of event.) Some of them will be bewildered, but most will get a sense of what dialogue is about and why it is important. Some people will need to enter this process intellectually. For them, we can provide an intellectual rationale of why intercultural events are important. Some people will enter this process only after they have discovered that there are issues they have to address. Their reaction may be more intense and may be very negative. This is when we must sanctify the fire right away, or they will leave the event with their fear confirmed and will be reluctant to return. We need to demonstrate to them that there is a constructive way to deal with intercultural issues. We don't have to light the unholy fire that will consume each other with accusation and judgment. Instead, we can show them the fire of Pentecost, where we speak in tongues to demonstrate what constructive dialogue looks, sounds, and feels like. Some may think that we are drunk, but for those who are amazed, they are ready to sanctify the fire with us by committing to do dialogue.

Sometimes the fire is already lit and people will gather if we provide the opportunities for them. For example, right after the 1992 Los Angeles riots, the Episcopal diocese invited me to put together an intercultural worship experience. With minimal publicity, the first service was attended by more than two hundred people. Out of this one-day worship experience, we were able to invite participants to join a smaller dialogue group to further discuss the issues raised by the riot. (See Appendices A and B for the full description of a similar worship service and intercultural dialogue program.)

Sanctifying the Fire

When the fire is lit, we must simultaneously sanctify it, or the unholy fire will take over. In order to prepare people for dialogue, we must create a safe and nonjudgmental environment. Be aware of the space in which the participants will interact. Different spaces have a different "spirit" residing in them. If we don't intentionally do something about the space, such as removing or putting up artifacts and rearranging the sitting configuration, the spirit of the space will take over. This spirit may or may not be helpful to the dialogue process. For example, I taught a college-level course that incorporated the intercultural dialogue process in each class. However, we were confined to a conventional classroom space, and it was very difficult to create a safe and comfortable environment, because there was a lot of traditional teaching mentality implicit in it. Whenever we engaged in a dialogue activity, we changed the configuration of the chairs from being in rows to a circle. We also put up posters of our communication ground rules on the wall. Summaries of dialogue shared in the previous class were transcribed onto a large piece of paper and posted on the chalkboards. Beyond the space, establishing communication ground rules, giving clear behavioral instruction, and establishing trust among the participants are all essential steps to creating a safe and nonjudgmental environment for dialogue.

Before doing anything that involves interaction among participants, a set of communication ground rules must be presented and agreed upon by everyone. We, people from different cultural backgrounds, bring with us different assumptions of communication styles. The cultural variables that affect the communication process mostly are high- and low-context communication styles[1] and power distance.[2] Sometimes these different assumptions can cause conflict and communication breakdowns.

---

[1] See chapter 11 for a full discussion on high- and low-context communication styles and their impact on the dialogue process.

[2] See Eric H. F. Law, *The Wolf Shall Dwell with the Lamb* (St. Louis: Chalice Press, 1993), pp. 13–36.

I have provided two sets of ground rules that I have developed and use frequently. The first set *(Figure 10.1 on page 86)* is written in narrative form to be read aloud at the beginning of a dialogue session. The second set *(Figure 10.2 on page 87)* is written with the acronym for the word "RESPECT." This set is more appropriate for putting on a large chart and displaying in the dialogue space. Also, the second set will require a more extensive discussion in order for the participants to gain a deeper understanding of what these guidelines mean in terms of behavior. Here are examples of two typical questions I would ask :

> What does it mean to "take responsibility for what you say and feel without blaming others"? What does it sound like when we are speaking to each other?

As participants respond to these questions, I elicit from them more concrete examples. For this particular ground rule, a participant may bring up the usage of "I" statements as a way of taking responsibility for what one says. Another participant may add, "That means to stop, to think about why I feel a certain way before I speak." The response will lead naturally to the discussion on the ground rules: Ponder what you hear and feel before you speak. The discussion on the ground rules should lead the participants to understand why ground rules are important. They are like a temporary covenant for the time and space in which the dialogue session takes place. Ground rules can prevent unnecessary accusatory arguments that are not productive for ensuring a safe environment in which participants can be honest and open. By the time the argument and accusation has started, it is too late to set ground rules. If we take great care in making sure that the ground rules are presented and affirmed before every activity or discussion, the group will take responsibility, reminding the participants about the ground rules when there is a conflict. The facilitator may then invite the participants to practice the ground rules by, for example, restating their point of view without blaming others or implying that the other point of view is wrong.

To ensure a safe environment for participants to share personal information, the facilitator and the participants commit to keeping confidentiality. This means that the personal information shared in the group stays in the group unless one has the permission of the speaker to share it with outsiders. This ground rule is crucial to provide safety for participants. This gives the participants the freedom to speak about things that might not be perceived as acceptable, such as admitting that one has prejudice, or expressing one's personal experience of discrimination.

Without the safety of confidentiality, people will hesitate to climb down from their towers of ethnocentrism, and to examine and share their biases.

I have also included a version of the ground rules in the form of a litany in Appendix A. By putting the ground rules in a theological context, we emphasize even more intentionally that the ground rules are the sanctifying agent for the dialogue process. Ground rules are like the holy fire around which people gather. They invite people to listen openly and speak honestly without being judgmental. They invite people to look inward first—to examine their own assumptions and perceptions—before engaging in conversation. "First take the log out of your own eye, and then you will see clearly to take the speck out of your neighbor's eye" (Luke 6:42). They sanctify the dialogue space by declaring right from the start that there is no right or wrong, good or bad. They create a level ground on which people can interact with each other equally. They take into account the differences in communication styles that might create an imbalance of power. Communication ground rules form a temporary covenant by which people abide as they gather around the burning bush. However, we must not fall into the trap of making the ground rules into a golden calf by making them into absolutes and use them to exclude and judge others. Ground rules simply describe the covenant relationship as best as it can be done in written form. Whenever ground rules are presented, they must be presented in a way that captures the essence of the covenant. These dialogue ground rules must be open to addition and modification as the community evolves and grows.

Maintaining the Holy Fire

After we have sanctified the fire, we must keep the holy fire burning. The ground rules will continue to keep a non-judgmental and safe environment if we review them at every gathering. But ground rules by themselves are not going to keep the holy fire burning. We, in our fear of uncertainty, will want to create a golden calf if we do not continue our intentional work of tending and caring for the holy fire.

Knowing when and how to use structured activities to enable participants to communicate honestly with each other is the next step. The conventional style of interaction, in which the leader asks a question and expects volunteers to offer their comments and questions, cannot be the only way that people participate. The difference in communication styles and perceptions of power

Figure 10.1
Communication Ground Rules[3]

1. We are *not* here to debate who is right or who is wrong. We are here to experience true dialogue in which we strive to communicate honestly and listen actively and openly to each other. We invite you to open your hearts and minds to experience new ideas, feelings, situations, and people, even though at times the process may be uncomfortable.

2. Our facilitators are not experts. Their role is to provide a structure and process by which we can better communicate with each other.

3. We recognize that we might have preconceived assumptions and perceptions about others—some are conscious; some are unconscious. We invite you to be aware of how they influence the way you listen and interpret others' words and actions. We also invite you to be aware of how these assumptions affect the way you speak and act in the group. In doing so, we can better maintain our respect for and acceptance of ourselves and others as valuable human beings.

4. We invite you to take responsibility for what you say and what you say on behalf of a group. We also invite you to speak with words that others can hear and understand and whenever possible, use specific personal examples that relate to the topic being discussed.

5. We invite you to expand your listening sense to include not just words, but also feelings being expressed, non-verbal communication such as body language, and different ways of using silence.

6. We invite you to take responsibility for your own feelings as they surface. Feelings may be triggered by particular words or actions, but they may or may not be directly related to the particular interaction. When this happens, simply communicate that feeling without blaming others. In doing so, members of the group can hear and learn constructively the consequences of their words and actions.

7. We invite you to hold the personal information shared here in confidence because only in this way can we feel free to say what is in our minds and hearts.

8. (Add this if translators are used.) If you are translating, try not to protect the speaker or the listener. Simply translate as truthfully as you can what the speaker is trying to say. It is all right to ask for help from others when there is a word or phrase of which you are not sure.

---

[3] A similar set of dialogue communication guidelines appears in my first book. I have added ground rule for translators. See Eric H. F. Law, *The Wolf Shall Dwell with the Lamb* (St. Louis: Chalice Press, 1993), pp. 104–106.

Figure 10.2

Respectful Communication Guidelines[4]

R = Take RESPONSIBILITY for what you say and feel without blaming others

E = EMPATHETIC listening

S = Be SENSITIVE to differences in communication styles

P = PONDER what you hear and feel before you speak

E = EXAMINE your own assumptions and perceptions

C = Keep CONFIDENTIALITY

T = TOLERATE ambiguity because we are *not* here to debate who is right or wrong

among the different cultural groups will precipitate an uneven verbal participation. The issue is that not all participants can volunteer their thoughts, or speak freely as individuals. While it is important to validate those participants who volunteer and speak freely by eliciting questions and comments after a presentation, we must also provide opportunities for the shier and quieter participants to express themselves. Structured activities can provide opportunities for small group sharing and intergroup interactions. These structured activities may include various kinds of group divisions, the use of the Mutual Invitation process, and the utilizing of group media such as flip-charts, work-sheets, and photographs.

Whenever we are involved in facilitating a structured activity, the instruction must be given in clear, concise, and behavioral terms. An instructions may be very clear in our mind as we give it, but it can be interpreted differently because of the participants' different cultural contexts. Giving clear, behavioral instructions will minimize the confusion and misunderstanding. For example, instead of giving the following nonbehavioral-specific instruction:

---

[4] The idea of putting the Communication Guidelines in this form came from a meeting I had with Jeanne Yeo-Ishikawa, Flora Rostamian, and Trilce Delgado in the summer of 1995. Around the same time Lucky Altman, of the National Conference, Los Angeles Region, came up with the same idea and created a different set of guidelines. Since the initial design of this set of guidelines, I have modified them a great deal based on my experience of using them in group dialogue work.

In your small groups, discuss the pros and cons of being a member of your cultural group.

Try giving clear behavioral instructions like this one instead:

In your small groups, first invite one person to record on the flip-chart. Then discuss and write down at least three concrete advantages of being a member of your cultural group and three issues that you face as a member of your cultural group. Before you return, elect a person to report the findings of your small group using the flip-chart. You have 20 minutes to do this.

In the first instructions, there is a lot of room for interpretation—how to report and what to report and who will give the report. The second set of instructions is more specific in terms of the expected behavior.

Another reason for giving clear behavioral instructions lies in the varying degree of tolerance of ambiguity that exists among the participants.[5] We can expect that some participants would be very comfortable entering an activity without knowing what is going to happen, while others would be extremely nervous and reluctant because of their low tolerance of ambiguity. The use of specific behavioral instructions provides more safety because it gives a clearer sense of what is going to happen before it happens. With a clearer expectation, the participants with a low tolerance of ambiguity can feel more at ease. All the dialogue processes described in the appendices incorporate this technique. Some of the activities require more precise behavioral instructions, based on past experience in facilitating the particular activity; therefore, the instructions are written in script form. They are written like a liturgy. The facilitator can simply read it. We will explore this "liturgical" form of leadership in depth in chapter 12. Bear in mind what behavior this set of instructions is supposed to produce, so that if there are questions, you can explain them further.

To further avoid misunderstandings or confusion regarding the expected behavioral outcome, the facilitator should always ask for feedback. "Are there any questions about what we are going to do?" The facilitator should be prepared to clarify any

---

[5] For a full discussion and research on cultural differences in tolerance of ambiguity which Hofstede called "Uncertainty Avoidance," see Geert Hofstede, *Culture's Consequences—International Differences in Work-Related Values,* abridged edition (Beverly Hills, London, New Delhi: Sage Publications, 1987), pp. 110–147.

part of the instructions when there are questions. This is why it is important for the facilitator to experience these activities first-hand before trying to facilitate it. Having firsthand experience, the facilitator can anticipate questions and address them more readily.

Because there will be participants with different perceptions of power, we cannot facilitate a discussion using only the volunteer style of interaction that favors those from individualistic cultures. Instead, we suggest that you use a very effective process called Mutual Invitation. Here is the description of the process as I would have given it in a group:

> *In order to ensure that everyone who wants to share has the opportunity to speak, we will proceed in the following way:*
>
> *The leader or a designated person will share first. After that person has spoken, he or she then invites another to share. Whomever you invite does not need to be the person next to you. After the next person has spoken, that person is given the privilege to invite another to share. If you don't want to say anything, simply say "pass," and proceed to invite another to share. We will do this until everyone has been invited.*[6]

I devoted a whole chapter in my previous book to analyzing why this process is an effective inclusive tool for managing a multicultural group. Therefore I will not explain this process in depth here. Even though this is a truly inclusive process, we cannot use this process for discussion all the time because we are always under the pressure of time limitations. For a group of about ten to fifteen people in a two-hour meeting, you can actually use Mutual Invitation at least three times at each meeting—beginning, midpoint, and toward the end. You can incorporate Mutual Invitation in the various activities and discussion topics. This way each participant is invited to give his/her input at least three times during every meeting.

When facilitating a discussion, specifically after an activity, the facilitator needs to provide opportunities for each participant to verbalize her learning. By articulating the learning, participants can remember it better and therefore can access this insight again more readily in the future. However, when the group size increases, the sharing time per participant decreases. It is a

---

[6] See Eric H. F. Law, *The Wolf Shall Dwell with the Lamb* (St Louis: Chalice Press, 1993), pp. 79–88.

case of simple mathematics. The facilitator must be aware of the size of the group. When you wish to give the participants more time to share, you may need to divide the group into smaller groups. The disadvantage is that when they are in their small groups, the facilitator will have less control over the group process. The facilitator will not be able to listen to each participant's sharing. The participants will not be able to gain insight from everyone in the group. To provide opportunities for the participants to gain a fuller perspective, you can invite each small group to summarize their discussion and report back to the larger gathering. Figure 10.3 summarizes the advantages and disadvantages of maintaining a large group as opposed to dividing up into smaller groups.

Think about what you want to accomplish with an activity and decide what group size to assume. Remember to give very clear behavioral instructions when dividing into groups, so that each participant will have a clear understanding of the behavioral expectations. Be sure to specify any process that you want the small group to use. For example, if you want them to use Mutual Invitation, make sure that each group understands that and, to ensure the invitation process will continue, appoint a person in each group to enforce it.

Division into smaller groups is essential to enable participants to climb down from their towers and share their perspectives in such a way that interpathy among the participants can take place. Group division is most effective when there are clearly defined affinity groups in the community. Affinity groups consist of members who share something in common that will make it safer to discuss a certain issue. For example, if we are facilitating a dialogue of gender issues, it would be appropriate to divide the group into a male and female group. The resulting reports from the affinity groups will be more honest and in-depth, allowing more likelihood that the information will be listened to interpathically. If we are facilitating a dialogue dealing with generational issues, affinity groups may be formed around age differences. If we are facilitating a dialogue on race and ethnicity, affinity groups may be formed around race and ethnicity.

Affinity groups can also be determined by self-assessment. For example, Appendix C describes a process by which participants assess their communication styles by rating themselves on a scale of 1 to 6—1 being very low context and 6 being very high context. After they have made their own self-assessments, they are divided into affinity groups according to their rating. The same can be done when dealing with race and ethnicity. We can invite

Figure 10.3

**Comparison Between a Large Group
and a Division into Smaller Groups**

Stay in large group	Divide into smaller groups
Participants hear input from everyone	Participants hear smaller samples of responses
Facilitator has more control over the process	Facilitator has less control over the process in small groups
Less time for participants to verbalize their learning	More time for participants to verbalize their learning
Less safety for participants to share personally	More safety for participants to share personally, especially when participants have built some affinity within the small groups
If not using Mutual Invitation, only a few participants get to share	More participants get to share
May create individual competitiveness	May create group competitiveness

participants to self-identify their own race or ethnicity or culture. Once they have shared the different "labels" of identification, they are invited to form affinity groups according to what they have heard. In such a process, we may have more than just affinity groups based on race, culture, or ethnicity. We must be open to accepting groups that have defined themselves as simply "human beings" or groups with mixed racial heritage, and so forth.

Group division is also an essential part of managing a bilingual dialogue process. The affinity group will be formed based on language. In their own language group, they can discuss freely and with ease the issues, and the report of what was shared in the small group will be translated so that the other groups can understand the perspective of each language group. (See Appendix D for a full treatment of techniques for running a bilingual gathering.) Nevertheless, the goal for group division is to hear from each group's unique perspective. We must take great care in explaining why the group division is necessary. Here is a list of reasons:

1. Even though we could fall into the danger of climbing up our own tower of ethnocentrism by separating into affinity groups, when participants have the opportunity to share in the safety of their affinity group, the information they produce will be more genuine and in-depth according to their particular context and perspective. To ensure we do not climb any higher in our towers, reporting back from the small groups is essential. Another reason for reporting is to allow for interpathic listening.

2. Dividing into affinity groups can allow participants to engage in intragroup dialogue which can help them gain a stronger understanding of their self- and group identity before engaging in intergroup dialogue.

3. By dividing into affinity groups and eliciting interpretations and perceptions from their specific perspectives, we are affirming our commitment to cultural pluralism. Understanding the context of each affinity group will help us see the bigger, more complete picture of the topic being discussed.

4. If a decision has to be made, after hearing from all the different perspectives, we can engage in the process of contextual evaluation from which we can make a more inclusive decision.

Beyond setting the ground rules and an effective use of invitation and group division, the creative use of group media is the essential technique to keeping the burning bush going. Group media are those that enhance interpersonal communication in a group. They give participants more tools to communicate beyond words. A group medium can be exercise work-sheets, flip-charts, drawings, drama, photographs, slides, posters, music, audio- and videotapes, and so on.[7] In my previous book, I devoted a whole chapter to this, so I am not going to go into great detail on the use of group media. However, I will discuss the use of media technologies not as a golden calf to avoid intercultural encounter, but to use them as group media to enhance the intercultural dialogue process. In order for media technologies to be useful in the dialogue process, we must recapture one of the original purposes of media technology—to extend our human ability to reach each other. For example, through the Internet, I am establishing an ongoing dialogue with

---

[7] See Eric H. F. Law, *The Wolf Shall Dwell with the Lamb* (St. Louis: Chalice Press, 1993), pp. 89–98.

my nephews and nieces who live on the other side of the continent. We would have never thought of writing each other by "snail mail," as they would call it. But with this technology, I am able to reach out to them and they are able to reach back in a real, connective way. "Photolanguage" is a prime example of using the technology of photography to empower each person to communicate emotively using a wealth of still-photo images and symbols. In a dialogue process, we must ensure that whatever technology we are using is distributed evenly to all participants. Technology represents power. We must be very careful not to allow technology to become a site for the unholy fire to fester.

Media technologies by themselves do not automatically foster dialogue; they need the dialogue process to become useful group media. Showing a video by itself is not a group medium, but having a facilitated discussion afterward that allows people to share their different perceptions of what they have seen makes this video a group medium. One time after I did Photolanguage[8] to facilitate a group on racism, a participant said, "But I know this tool doesn't work all the time. I was in another workshop, and it created more arguments and bad feelings among the people there."

I thought for a few seconds before I replied. "When you experienced this tool, did the facilitator use the process that I used?" The process I used included presentation of the ground rules, silent reflection time, and mutual invitation.

"No," she replied, and then a light bulb turned on in her head. After thinking a minute, she added, "I see."

Even a well-tested tool like Photolanguage by itself is not going to guarantee that the participants will engage in constructive dialogue. The technology of Photolanguage is effective only when it is used in the context of the dialogue process.

When the participants come out of an intense experience, the facilitator needs to help them gain a sense of closure before they leave—that is, to bring the participants back to their "safe zone," so that they do not feel like there is unfinished business when they leave. Unfinished business can be intense emotions that have not been dealt with appropriately, or tensions that have not been resolved. You do not want the participants to leave feeling resentful, hurt, or left out. Therefore plan and respect the time for closure when you are engaging in dialogue and experiential activities.

---

[8] For a full description of the process, see Eric H. F. Law, *The Wolf Shall Dwell with the Lamb* (St. Louis: Chalice Press, 1993), pp. 115–119.

Debriefing each activity is an essential step to help participants draw learning from the process. The facilitator should synthesize, recap, and restate learning that the participants arrived at during and after the activity. After the participants have had a chance to share what they have learned, invite them to go further by asking them how they would apply the learning to their lives and ministries. Then the next crucial step is to invite them to evaluate the session itself. How can they enact the positive aspects of this session when they gather again? How can they improve future gatherings? The facilitator must give great care in incorporating the suggestions and reflections into the dialogue process for the next gathering. In other words, every time we do a dialogue process, we invite the participants and the community to refine the process at the end. This will ensure that the process does not become static, but rather remains a process that evolves with the community. This will ensure that the dialogue process itself does not become a golden calf.

So far, I have covered all the essential techniques for facilitating a dialogue process. Here is a summary:

1. Set communication ground rules
2. Commit to confidentiality
3. Use structured activities
4. Give clear behavioral instructions
5. Invite feedback to make sure that the instruction is understood
6. Use Mutual Invitation
7. Use the group division technique
8. Use group media
9. Facilitate closure
10. Evaluate the process in order to improve future processes

Here is an example of how most of these "techniques" came together to help me in a highly volatile situation.

I was invited to consult with a committee of a large region of a major denomination. This particular region of the church was formerly two separate regions. A year before, the two regions decided to merge. In the process, two committees had to become one. One of the former regions had a very strong tradition of female leadership, and the population in this region had been mostly European Americans. The other region included a major city and had in the previous ten years been taking affirmative action very seriously. As a result, many African Americans, mostly male, were in leadership positions when the merger occurred. When the two committees merged, for whatever reason, the resulting chair of the new committee was a European-American woman and the vice chair was an African-American man. One year later, the chair was to be promoted to another ministry position and had to leave the post as the chair of this committee. In the following election, a European-American woman again was elected as the chair, while the African-American vice-chair remained in his position. Then, as they say, "all hell broke loose." The African-American community charged the committee with being racist, while the new leadership denied it by saying, "We followed due process." Letters flew back and forth between various groups and the bishop. Having heard and read all the complaints, the bishop decided to halt the process and asked the committee to hold a new election. The unholy fire was burning quite hot. It was on the verge of consuming not only individuals, but the institution in which this organization was housed. That was when I was called in to help. My charge was to help this group hold an election that would make everybody "happy." I was given two days to do this.

As a preparation to facilitate this event, I prayed. I prayed that I would not create a golden calf around which they would dance, resulting in some immediately good feelings but no dealings at all with the heart of the issue. I prayed that God would enter the fire with me to sanctify it so that they could gather around it to dialogue, instead of pronouncing judgment. With these prayerful thoughts in my mind, I proceeded to design this event. I decided that they would not be ready to make any decision until they had engaged in true dialogue with each other regarding the issues of race and gender. If I simply put myself in the role of the moderator of the election, they would just continue to fuel the unholy fire with more arguments and accusations. I was not willing to sit through two days of that sort of thing. But I knew that they would be impatient about not getting to the election sooner. I knew I could not give in to this obsession over the unholy fire, but had to use all the power that I could muster to create time and space for constructive dialogue.

I began the gathering with dialogue ground rules. We spent some time really digesting what it meant to follow these communication guidelines. I was trying to set up the nonjudgmental, safe space that I needed before they could dialogue with each other. I spent some time explaining to them why I would not get to the election until we had some time to do constructive dialogue, and for them to gain some new skills in communication.

Then I facilitated a few communication exercises and experiential activities that focused on the potential conflict caused by the different cultural perceptions of power and communication styles. I further emphasized that we might not be conscious of these different styles and perceptions within ourselves; therefore, we assumed others would think and perceive the same way. Using the cultural iceberg analogy,[9] I visually showed them that many conflicts happen below the water line on the unconscious, implicit level. The kinds of conflicts with which we were dealing on this committee were at this implicit level. We could not resolve these conflicts by a reelection, because the election was only the tip of the iceberg. To get at the heart of the conflict, we had to lower the water line to expose the jagged bottom of the iceberg, which was where the unconscious assumptions and values lay. This would mean examining our values and learning to communicate them with each other so that we could truly understand each other before trying to solve our problems.

Then we studied the Pentecost passage from Acts using the Community Bible Study[10] method, which incorporated ground rules again, and the use of Mutual Invitation. In this study we concentrated on speaking and listening and how they worked together in making the miracle of Pentecost a reality.[11] In this process, we theologically reaffirmed the need for open listening and honest speaking in our dialogue process. We were inviting God into our fire and affirming the presence of God in our midst. Now the burning bush was in place. I had sanctified the fire. We were ready for dialogue.

I invited the group to form affinity groups based on cultural differences. This, of course, caused a great deal of upheaval. After some clarification, there was an African-American group, a mixed-race women's group, a mixed gender and cultural group, a small Asian-American group, a very small Hispanic group, and a white male group. There were also a few individuals who did

---

[9] For a fuller discussion on internal and external cultures using the iceberg analogy, see Eric H. F. Law, *The Wolf Shall Dwell with the Lamb* (St. Louis: Chalice Press, 1993), pp. 4–10.

[10] See Appendix A for the questions used in studying the Pentecost passage. For a full description of the Community Bible Study process, see Eric H. F. Law, *The Wolf Shall Dwell with the Lamb* (St. Louis: Chalice Press, 1993), pp. 121–131.

[11] For a full discussion on the Pentecost passage, see Eric H. F. Law, *The Wolf Shall Dwell with the Lamb* (St. Louis: Chalice Press, 1993), pp. 45–53.

not want to be in any group at all. In their groups, they were asked to discuss and record their answers to the following question:

> As a member of my cultural group, what is it like being a leader of this church?
>
>> List three advantages;
>> List three contributions; and
>> List three struggles.

When they returned, many expressed their negative feelings toward being separated from others, while others felt that the opportunity to share with our "own" group was a welcome change. We discussed why there was a difference in perception about the group division process. An Asian American said, "When I am in a mixed group, I can't seem to get a word in."

A European American said, "I guess I was always taught that it is bad to separate from others, especially minorities. That's not a politically correct thing to do."

"I just enjoyed speaking in my own language for a change. I can express myself better, and I can talk about my feelings knowing that the others can fully understand me."

"I feel an overwhelming sense of loss. I worked very hard in the sixties to integrate with minorities. I just can't deal with the fact that we have to segregate ourselves again. Was all my work in vain?"

There were many other comments but there was also listening. Real listening on the part of many people in the group—*interpathy*. After we debriefed the process, they shared the content of their reports. As they continued to listen to each other, they began to pinpoint from where the conflict came. They discovered that the women had had a hard time attaining leadership positions in the past because of the sexist system of the church. Their leadership roles in the former conference was an achievement they cherished as a sign of constructive change in the church system. From the reports, they also learned that the African-American community expected that the vice-chair would automatically move into the chair position when the chair resigned her position. They began to understand that this was a part of their culture, in which respect was given to seniority. When the promotion did not happen, they felt that it was disrespectful of the authority of the African American in the vice-chair position. As the African-American members voiced their complaints, the women felt that they might lose their gain for which they had worked so hard. So they fought back, holding firm to their ground, because they would not give in to allowing a man to "take over" again. They climbed higher onto their towers. Feeling the resistance to change, the African-American members also climbed a level higher in their towers by accusing the committee of being racist.

Having understood the conflict from these different perspectives, they were now ready to develop a new covenant from which they could respect each other while they were doing their work. I basically asked them to evaluate their dialogue with each other so far, and learn from the positive elements, and to figure out how these elements could continue to enhance their experience together. I invited them to form small groups—this time in mixed groups, to determine what would be an appropriate set of community principles that the committee should affirm in order to function. They went into groups and then reported back. After the reports, it was pretty clear that they wanted to reaffirm the ground rules that I had used at the beginning of the event. Furthermore, they would continue to explore how to use the Mutual Invitation process and the group division technique as new ways for them to interact with each other. Now they were ready for the election.

I worked with the outgoing chair and designed a process through which the committee could arrive at a nomination and election. Here is the outline:

1. Review dialogue ground rules.
2. Open the floor for general discussion on issues regarding the nomination.
3. Twenty minutes for people to volunteer their thoughts.
4. Twenty minutes for people to invite each other to share their thoughts.
5. Invite people to go into affinity groups that would be relevant to the nomination for twenty minutes.
6. When the groups return the floor is open for nominations.
7. When nominations are closed, the election is held.

This process worked very well. In the first twenty minutes, the ones who normally spoke out in the groups shared their ideas and concerns readily. In the next twenty minutes, the participants were careful to invite those who had not spoken. A few of them passed because what they wanted to say was already said, but many spoke eloquently on the issues. If they had not incorporated the invitation in the process, they would have missed these valuable inputs. In the affinity group process, this time there were no complaints—in fact, there was a sense of acceptance that it was all right to go into a group of people with whom they could talk freely about this particular issue. The groups were formed quickly, and they ended up in ethnic and gender groups. It was also interesting to observe that many did not want or need to go into small groups, so they just took a break from the meeting. After the affinity group discussion, they were ready to reap the fruits of their two days of hard work. When the floor was open for nominations, almost each affinity group presented a name. These names fitted the different offices of the committee. When the nominations were closed, there was only one name per office, and the nomination and the election was done. When the chair asked the gathering whether they would be happy with this list, they all agreed. They were utterly amazed at how fast they accomplished this task, which, two days ago, seemed so hopeless. The new chair, incidentally, was neither a European-American woman nor an African-American man. The committee had decided collectively, after hearing all the perspectives, to elect an Asian American to chair the committee. This was a choice that both sides could live with. Then they prayed, sang, and thanked God for leading them through this process. I, too, thanked God for being with me in the fire. The burning bush was at work and the fire did not consume.

CHAPTER ELEVEN

Differences in Communication Styles and the Dialogue Process

The works of cultural anthropologists have been a great resource for my ministry in understanding and designing dialogue processes that can move a group of people closer to becoming a multicultural community. For example, in *The Wolf Shall Dwell with the Lamb*, I drew from the work of Greet Hofstede on Power Distance, which explained why there is a uneven power distribution at most intercultural gatherings. Based on his work, I created the Mutual Invitation process as a dialogue tool that would enable group members to communicate with each other with equal power and opportunity. In further reflection on the dialogue process, I found Edward T. Hall's work on the difference between high- and low-context cultures most useful, specifically in the area of different communication styles.[1] I believe understanding his work will enable us to design and facilitate dialogue processes that are more sensitive to the different communication styles that exist in different cultural groups.

The goal of communication, whether we are the sender or the receiver, is to arrive at a common meaning. In order to have meaning, one must be aware of the various contexts: the external context of the situation and the internal contexts of the sender and the receiver. The external context of the situation may include the physical environment and the roles of the communica-

---

[1]See Edward T. Hall, *Beyond Culture* (New York, London, Toronto, Sydney, Auckland: An Anchor Press Book, Doubleday, 1976), pp. 85–116.

tors: for example, a verbal message of "I'm very hot" can have different meanings depending on the context in which it is said. If it is said in the context of a very hot and humid day, it may be a statement of the physical condition. If it is said in the context of two persons flirting with each other, it may imply sexual arousal. If it is said in a hospital, the sender may be indicating that he or she is seriously ill with a fever.

The internal contexts of both the sender and the receiver include their social, spiritual, and cultural environments. These are the beliefs, values, thought patterns, and myths imbedded in the internal cultures of the communicators. One function of our internal context is to provide a selective screen between ourselves and the environment designating what we pay attention to and what we ignore. Because our internal contexts are different, we may pay attention to or ignore different things in the same environment, therefore leading us to different interpretations. For example, three people went to see a play in which the two principal characters argued emotionally over the issue of racial discrimination. An African American may see the play as a testimony of the experiences of discrimination suffered by African Americans. A white American may see the play as a white-bashing political statement. A person who grew up with parents who argued all the time may simply shut down and leave the play without hearing its substance at all. Depending on our internal contexts, we may observe, react, and perceive very different meanings in the same situation. To achieve effective communication, people with different internal contexts must spend time and energy in establishing a common context in which they can arrive at a common meaning. This is what Hall called "contexting."

"Contexting" or building a common context is a way of avoiding information overload. By establishing a common context, the communicators can screen out the shared information and focus on the message being transmitted efficiently and economically. For example, the years of theological training for priests, pastors, and lay ministers where they learned the common theological language are, in this sense, building this common context so that when these professionals interact together, they can understand each other efficiently and effectively without having to explain every term each time. In the same way, this book has been a contexting medium between you, the reader, and me; by the time you get to this chapter, you know what I mean when I use terms such as "the burning bush," "golden calf," "tower of ethnocentrism," "ethnorelativism," etc., without having them explained in detail again.

The more context we share in a system (high-context), the more stability we have. The less context we share (low-context), the more changes can occur in the system. In other words, when we need to adapt and change, we have to move toward a low-context style of relating because we have to acquire new information and cannot rely on preprogrammed information. In the process of "reprogramming," we have to explicitly code all the information so that we can learn with full understanding. On the other hand, when there is a need of stability, we tend to move toward a high-context style of relating because the tradition is established and everyone is preprogrammed to understand the tradition without its being explained every time. The more this tradition becomes implicit, the less likely that it will be changed.[2]

Let us apply the concept of context to cultural differences. Hall asserts that a major difference between cultures is the degree in which a cultural group relies on this context in communication. He ranked this continuum, from a high-context culture to a low-context culture.

In high-context cultures, people are deeply involved with each other and they strongly value the collectiveness of their community. When people communicate, "most of the information is either in the physical context or internalized in the person, while very little is in the coded, explicit, transmitted part of the message."[3] Simple messages can have deep meaning. In a high-context culture, the communication system itself is frequently used as an art form. High-context culture tends to be rooted in the past. Knowing the long tradition is part of the programming required in order to communicate effectively. Since tradition is valued highly, change is slow and sometimes difficult. People in authority are expected to be the keepers of tradition and are personally and truly responsible for the actions of all their subordinates. Since people have very strong bonds with each other, they also allow for considerable bending of the system to accommodate deviation from tradition while maintaining its stability.

In communication, a sender expects the receiver to know the message without its being specific. The message transmitted contains minimal explicit information. This can come in two forms. They may use a lot of nonverbal communication such as body language, or they may talk around the subject without ever getting to the point. Effective communication relies heavily on

---

[2] For a full treatment on "Context and Meaning," see chapter 6 of Edward T. Hall, *Beyond Culture*, pp. 85–104.
[3] See Edward T. Hall, *Beyond Culture*, p. 91.

preprogrammed information (the internal context) in the receiver and in the environment. In order for effective communication to take place, time must be devoted to programming each person within the culture, or communication will not be complete. Therefore, it is very easy to make distinctions between insiders and outsiders because insiders can communicate efficiently, economically and with much satisfaction while outsiders, without the pre-programming to understand the minimal messages, would be at a loss. A high-context system may appear to be exclusive initially because of this. One has to realize that it takes a substantial amount of time for contexting with this system before one can be fully accepted.

While people from high-context systems can be very creative in their own environment, they are very inefficient in dealing with anything new. Since any new situation requires them to move to the low-context side of relating in order for them to start building a common context, a high-context person will require more detailed information and instruction, and therefore take more time to arrive at a comfortable level of shared context in order to function with ease. They need more context time.

Low-context cultures tend to be highly individualized. Most people relate to each other tangentially and tend not to be deeply involved with others. Since they don't share or expect to share a common context with each other when they communicate, they put most of the information in the transmitted message in order to make up for what is missing in the context. They highly value the explicit code, usually spoken or written, as the dominant means of communication and may pay less attention to implicit information imbedded in the communicator's context and in the environment.

Being people from low-context systems does not mean that they do not have a cultural context. It means they still have a context with its selective screen, except that low-context people are less aware of their context and sometimes assume that it does not exist. As a result, they tend to look for and apply universal rules and values to everybody and do not make a great distinction between insiders and outsiders. Sometimes, what they perceive as universal values may not be universal at all and may just be part of their own internal context. Low-context systems may appear to be very inclusive at first because of their openness, without requiring any contexting time in order to relate to someone. The paradox is that they do exclude others, perhaps unintentionally, when they expect everyone to be low-context like them.

Since people do not have strong ties with each other or with organizations, based on whether or not things are going well for them, they may move in and out of organizations and relationships with ease and without guilt. Organizational coherence depends not on individual persons in authority, since that can change rapidly, but on the system. Responsibility is diffused through the system and difficult to pin down. People expect the system to protect its members. Low-context systems emphasize the present and future and can be changed easily and rapidly to adapt to new situations. Such a system may also be more vulnerable to manipulation.

People from low-context systems are very creative and innovative when dealing with something new. They can confront new situations without requiring a great amount of time and detailed programming. They do not need a lot of "contexting" time. However, they may have trouble understanding and functioning in a high-context environment since they are less aware of the screen they have within themselves, let alone being aware of the highly selective screen that high-context people have.[4]

When a conflict occurs, low-context persons favor an open, direct, and confrontational style. They believe conflict can be resolved by revealing all the facts with all parties involved being honest and explicit about their experiences and feelings. Once everything is "out in the open," they believe they can find a solution, which is often action-oriented. High-context persons, on the other hand, prefer an ambiguous, indirect, and non-confrontational approach. Since the relationship and cohesion of the group is highest in their priorities, they believe that direct confrontation would be too damaging to the stability of the organization and relationship. They employ "face saving" strategies that emphasize the importance of maintaining the relationship. The parties involved are expected to read the implicit message—"I'm hurt" or "I'm sorry"—without its being specific. We can see the potential problems presented by this different style of managing conflict. See Figure Four for a summary of the characteristics of high- and low-context communication styles.

In an intercultural encounter, low-context people will be the direct, confrontational, and talkative ones. While they require little time to move right into the task at hand, high-context people are still taking their time for "contexting." High-context people want to know what is the context of the situation and

---

[4] For a full description of high- and low-context culture, see chapter 7 of Edward T. Hall, *Beyond Culture*, pp. 105–116.

where they stand in relation to others before they can function effectively. Furthermore, in order for high-context people to engage in dialogue, they need to trust the group, and developing this trust takes time. Meanwhile, before the trust building can even begin, the low-context people are ready to discuss the issues. They light the fire without being aware of the high-context people's readiness to do this. When they start talking and being very direct, the high-context people, without a common, trusting context, retreat to their indirect, concealing strategies in order to protect themselves. The more the low-context people push and confront, the more the high-context people retreat.

Then the judgment comes. "Why can't they be honest and tell the truth? Why don't they want to find a solution to the problem? I can't read their minds! Why are they so passive-aggressive?" The unholy fire is blazing by now. With this judgmental confrontation, the high-context people retreat even more and may stop responding altogether. When there is a break from the meeting, they retreat to the comfort of their own collective by gathering and talking with people from their own community. More judgment comes from the low-context people. "Why are they so exclusive? They are going back to segregation again." If a decision needs to be made, the low-context people get very frustrated with what they consider the "nonresponsive" and "nonparticipatory" attitudes of the others and make the decision themselves without truly understanding the others' perspective.

If we do a power analysis, the low-context people, by behaving the way they have been taught to be good communicators, tend to dominate the discussion verbally and eventually the decision-making process. The high-context people become powerless because they never got the chance to develop any context from which they could operate. In the end, the high-context people get blamed for the failure to communicate in the encounter. How can we do justice in a ethnorelative way in this situation? How can we construct an environment in which high- and low-context people can communicate with equal power? How can we design our dialogue processes to sanctify this unholy fire?

The following is a list of dialogue techniques that I would emphasize when there are both high- and low-context communicators in the group:

1. Provide "contexting" time in exploring and modifying communication ground rules.
2. Help people explore their communication styles and the consequences when interacting with others who have a different style.

Figure 11.1
Characteristics of
Low- and High-Context Communication Styles

High-Context	Low-Context
group-oriented	individual-oriented
rely heavily on the physical context or the shared context of the transmitter and receiver; very little is in the coded, explicit, transmitted part of the message	rely on explicit coding of information being communicated; less aware of contexts
spiral logic	linear logic
take time for "contexting" in new situation	adjust to new situation quickly
conflict may occur because of violations of collective expectations	conflict may occur because of violations of individual expectations
deal with conflict by concealment	deal with conflict by revealment
indirect, nonconfrontational attitude	direct, confrontational attitude
"face" saving	fact finding
focus on relationship	focus on action and solution
ambiguous, indirect strategies	open, direct strategies

3. Use the Mutual Invitation process to even out the power distribution.

4. Use the Group Division technique to allow for the need to share in their own cultural context.

5. Use Group Media to help people express themselves more clearly and concretely.

In the process of sanctifying the fire, we must present the dialogue communication guidelines as a "contexting" process. Invite participants to reflect on their style of communication and share it with the rest of the group. A typical process may involve a sequence of questions as follows:

1. What do I have to do to get here?

2. What gifts do I bring to this gathering?

3. What do others need to know about me/us in order for me/us to function or communicate effectively in this gathering?

4. How do I know I am being respected?

5. Based on answers to the last two questions, what are my/our responsibilities in order for the gathering to be inclusive and respectful of everyone?

6. What are some community ground rules and policies that we need to affirm?

At the beginning of the dialogue session, the facilitator can set the initial communication ground rules. Invite the participants to answer these questions progressively one at a time by using different techniques. For example, for questions one and two, we can use the Mutual Invitation process. For questions three and four, we can divide participants into affinity groups to discuss and report back. For questions five and six, we can invite them to write their answers on a large piece of paper (a group medium) taped on the wall for all to see. At the end of the process, the participants are asked to review the communication ground rules and make suggestions for modification and addition. This is a process that combines setting the ground rules and providing contexting time. The end product of this process is a deeper understanding of why we need communication ground rules, but while they are accomplishing that, they are also getting to know and building trust with each other.

One of the standard communication ground rules that I use is "Be sensitive to differences in communication styles." In order to help participants to honor this ground rule, communication style itself can be a dialogue topic. The following is an outline of the dialogue process that I have used effectively to help people understand the difference between high- and low-context communication styles. Furthermore, this process also assists the participants in making constructive personal adjustments in order to better communicate with others. (See Appendix C for a full description of the process.)

1. Present the different characteristics of high- and low-context styles of communication.
2. Invite participants to rate themselves on a scale of 1 to 6, 1 being very low-context and 6 being very high-context.
3. Divide participants into small groups according to their self-assessment.
4. These small groups should discuss and record what they consider to be three potential problems when they are communicating with people from the other side of the high-low context continuum, and then arrive at three self-adjustments that would address these potential problems constructively.
5. Invite each group to report back to the large group.
6. Invite participants to dialogue on whether each group's self-adjustments would work and invite modification and enhancement.
7. Review communication ground rules and invite participants to add or modify them based on what they had learned from this dialogue process.

This process employs the group division technique to allow for more in-depth sharing. It supports the commitment to cultural pluralism. It affirms that there is more than one style of communication and these styles are not good or bad, they are just different. It also provides time for high-context people to share among themselves and develop a trustful context while giving the low-context people a task that is direct and to the point. At the end of this process, the group is then asked again what would be some community communication guidelines that would be important for this group to uphold in order for them to continue to communicate with each other effectively. Using the terminology that we have developed in the previous chapters, in this dialogue process, we invite people to climb down from their tower, examining their own context, in this case, their communication styles. By the time they land on the ground, they have gained a deeper knowledge of their own communication styles. On the ground, they gather around the burning bush and acknowledge their strengths and weaknesses when they communicate with each other. In their dialogue around the holy fire, they create a new context that they share—a new covenant—with which they can better respect each other when they communicate.

I was invited to facilitate an intergenerational dialogue for a Chinese congregation. Half the group who came to this day-long event were first-generation immigrants (mostly Chinese speaking) and the other half were second-generation Chinese Americans (mostly English-speaking). The goal of the day was to help the two groups to communicate and understand each other more across the cultural and language barrier. My assessment of the situation was that there was not only a language barrier, but there was also a major difference in their styles of communication. The first-generation Chinese Americans were more high-context. Their complaints about their children, the second generation, were that they were rude, pushy, and didn't respect their family tradition. The second-generation Chinese Americans were educated in the United States and had learned to be very low-context in order to survive. Their complaints about their parents were that they were stubborn, controlling, and did not show their feelings. With the difference in communication styles, even when the language barrier is overcome with translation, there will still be an imbalance of verbal participation. Add to this the differences in perception of power and authority between the generations; communication that leads to a common meaning is even harder to achieve without the intentional dialogue process.

The first step of the dialogue process was to help this group build a common context with which they could communicate with each other. The bilingual issue was easy to deal with; I just followed the basic techniques that I had developed. (See Appendix G—Technique for Managing a Bilingual Gathering.) After setting the ground rules in two languages, I invited them to practice how to communicate across language barriers. I added a new element to the Mutual Invitation process in order for the bilingual dialogue to take place. After a person was invited to speak, he or she, depending on his or her language ability, could invite a bilingual person to translate. There were about five bilingual participants with varying degrees of language proficiency. Of course, if the bilingual person who had been invited to translate was not willing to do it, he/she could say, "Pass." By this time, they had filled in a wall chart[5] with the following topics:

---

[5]This process is called "Conocimientos." See Appendix B for a full description.

1. Name
2. Birthplace
3. Languages that I speak
4. One value I learned from my parents that I would pass on to the next generation
5. One value I would not pass on to the next generation

The responses were written in the language of their choice. I invited them to share what they wrote on the chart using the Mutual Invitation process with the added translation option. They struggled with the process at first, but once they got used to it, it became more like a normal activity. What actually happened was that at any one time, two persons would work as a team to help one of the team members communicate with the whole group. If the translator had a word or phrase that she might not know how to translate, the translator asked the other translators to help. As they moved along in this contexting time, they saw that the whole community, young and old, speaking in Chinese and English, took the responsibility to help each person communicate what was on his or her mind. At the end of the introductory process, they realized that they could really trust and rely on each other as they moved toward the next activity.

Then I put them into two small groups by language preference—a Chinese-speaking group and an English-speaking group. Each group was given a set of Photolanguage. Using the standard process, each person picked one or two pictures to describe what it was like to be a Chinese American. Each group shared their photos in their own language group. Then one bilingual person in each group was invited to report back to the other group using all the photos selected by his group. The English-speaking group's report focused on two issues: the difficulty living in two cultures, and the problem of finding a mate. The Chinese-speaking group's report focused mostly on the loss they felt when they came to the United States. They missed their way of life back in Hong Kong or China. As a result they would do anything to hold on to anything that would give them that feeling of being connected to their native land. For the first time the second-generation participants understood why their parents were so "controlling," while the first-generation participants understood the issues and pain that their children faced in the United States. As a result, they no longer pointed their fingers at each other and blamed each other for their problems. The fire was sanctified and they finally sat down around the burning bush truly communicating and understanding each other. Furthermore, they began to explore how they could continue to communicate with each other clearly and respectfully like they had done in the day-long program. They left with hope and excitement that there was a way to communicate respectfully across language and generational barriers.

The existence of the high- low-context continuum in the way different cultural groups communicate definitely affirms and supports the dialogue techniques that I have presented so far. The dialogue process always starts as a low-context process because we cannot assume all the participants share the same internal cultural context. However, we cannot simply function in a low-context way that will exclude the high-context communicators. How do we facilitate a dialogue that enables participants to express their thoughts and feelings without putting people from high-context cultures at a disadvantage? In the example described above, spending the time to do "contexting" was essential in building that initial trust that the high-context communicators needed. Dividing into language groups gave each group the comfort it needed to share in an honest and open way. This is especially important in giving the high-context communicators the opportunity to discuss the issue in its own context. To further enable the high-context groups to communicate with each other, I used the group media Photolanguage, allowing them to share their feelings in a more concrete and revealing way.

Even though a dialogue process begins as a low-context process, we must quickly help the participants to move to a higher-context level of participation by building a new common context. We do this by setting the communication ground rules and enabling them to build a trusting community. As shown in the example above, as the group struggled with the new context for communication using the method of inviting a translating partner, their comfort level with the process increased. As this new common context builds, the participants can feel more and more at ease in communicating their thoughts and feelings with each other. By the time we got to the Photolanguage activity, they were communicating in a new high-context way. It is at this level of communication that the participants can feel safe to challenge each other to change and grow. It is at the high-context level of communication that the participants can share and listen interpathically to each other. We must strive to attain this high-context level of communication in each dialogue process.

CHAPTER TWELVE

Dialogue as Liturgy

Remove the sandals from your feet, for the place on
which you are standing is holy ground.
—Exodus 3:5

Moses saw that the bush was blazing but was not consumed, an extraordinary phenomenon. In this unnatural oc-
currence, Moses recognized the presence of God in the burning
bush and took off his sandals. Removing one's sandals is a
deliberate, respectful act acknowledging the presence of God.
When we recognize the presence of God, we hear God's command, as Moses did, and we respond by doing the work of
justice. The act of doing something intentional becomes the
visible sign of the presence of God, who otherwise would be
invisible. Jesus said at the Last Supper, "Do this in remembrance
of me." In the liturgy of the Eucharist, we act deliberately to
prepare ourselves for worship through prayers and hymn singing.
We continue our deliberate acts by reading and reflecting on the
Holy Scriptures, through which we hear the Word of God. Then
we respond by confessing our sins and reconciling with our
neighbors, through the passing of the peace and the offering of
ourselves and our gifts to God. Finally we reenact what Jesus did
in the Last Supper by the breaking of the bread and the blessing
of the wine. In these deliberate acts, the presence of God through
Christ is made known to all who participate. This does not mean
that our liturgical acts can evoke the presence of God. God is
present with us at all times. Our liturgical acts simply let God's
presence be known. When we act intentionally, we are no longer
simply reacting based on our own assumptions and values. In the
liturgy, we force ourselves to acknowledge the presence of God
and take God's values into account.

Dialogue is a deliberate act. In our everyday interaction with our family, friends, and coworkers, we act "naturally" without thinking about how we are perceived by others. Only when there is a conflict may we stop to examine our values and beliefs. Most of the time, we just act and react. We don't think about communication ground rules when we talk to someone casually. We don't think about using group media. We don't think about how to divide people into small groups so that they can talk in more in-depth and honest ways. These dialogue techniques can be considered as "unnatural" acts. In a society where the win/lose mentality permeates everything that we do, the dialogue process is definitely an unnatural phenomenon. Dialogue as a deliberate act can be considered a liturgy. There are advantages in treating dialogue as a liturgy. First, liturgy employs a form-centered style of leadership. Second, liturgy is something that people reenact regularly. Third, liturgy is God-centered. I will examine why these three elements of liturgy are so important to the dialogue process.

1. Liturgy employs a form-centered style of leadership.

Dialogue processes, as defined by the last two chapters, require certain facilitative skills that a community leader may or may not have. However, I am not willing to make the skill and sensitivity requirement into a golden calf, excluding people who want to develop a multicultural community. I began to explore what other ways there are of providing leadership to develop a multicultural community through dialogue. I discovered one of my assumptions that was blocking me from moving toward an alternative leadership model was that leadership resides in a person. As long as I perceived that leadership depended on the skill of the individual leader, I was stuck with the golden calf, excluding persons who did not have the "skill level" to manage a multicultural community. This expectation of person-centered leadership was the cause of the rise and fall of many ministries, depending on who was leading them. I have observed that often a multicultural community gathered around a gifted leader who had the commitment and skill to hold the community together. The community fell apart, though, when the leader left, because the new leader did not hold the same commitment or have the same set of skills. The fate of a multicultural community is too important to leave up to one or two individuals.

As I let go of my golden calf, I began to experiment with a new style of dialogue facilitation that was based on liturgical forms. As an Episcopalian, I grew up with the Book of Common

Prayer, which lays out all the liturgies used by the church in fine detail, but allows for a great deal of flexibility. The content of each liturgy is different in terms of the hymns, scriptural readings, and sermons, but the form remains the same. The form is recognized and upheld by the community. When an individual leader strays from this form, the community would know. Liturgy employs a form-centered leadership in which the form itself is the leader, not the individual leader.

With this concept of form-centered leadership, I began to write out the dialogue process as if it were a liturgy. The dialogue processes included in the appendices are some examples of the dialogue process written out like a liturgy. With the process written out in such detail, I no longer require a facilitator with a very high skill level in order to implement a dialogue process. All I have to do is to teach the facilitators to respect and trust the process and know how to read in a way that makes the process come alive.

When I was invited to train facilitators to implement a five-session intercultural dialogue program for the whole Episcopal Diocese of Los Angeles right after the 1992 riots, I struggled with how to train a large number of competent facilitators in a short time. If I relied on the person-centered leadership style, I would have to spend at least a week to train every fifteen facilitators. This was not possible in terms of my time and the time commitment available from the volunteers. I decided to transform the dialogue processes into five liturgies. I wrote out each process in fine detail, in script form. The training program consisted of some basic facilitation skills such as using Mutual Invitation, setting the dialogue ground rules, and explaining how to use Group Media. The rest of the training involved each facilitator's practicing how to read each liturgy, allowing it to come alive for the group. With only twelve hours of training, the facilitators were confident in implementing the dialogue process. By transforming the dialogue process into a liturgical form, I also allowed it to be propagated faster, even though the varying skill levels of the facilitators may cause the dialogue process to be inconsistent from one group to another. But nevertheless, with the limitation, I believe by doing dialogue in a liturgical form, we can impart it to more people in the long run.

2. Liturgy is something that people reenact regularly.

Dialogue is not a one-time deal. Engaging in intercultural dialogue is a lifetime process. Each time I engage in a dialogue with someone who is different, I learn something new about myself and I appreciate the values and beliefs of the other person more. Many organizations invite me to give a workshop on interracial/intercultural issues, yet give me only three hours. The assumption behind these requests is that everyone who attends the workshop can become culturally sensitive via a one-time fix. My response to these requests is that it cannot be done. In such a short time, I can give them a taste of what it is like to address these issues constructively, but it will take a lot more time if they are serious about increasing the intercultural sensitivity of the people in their organization.

Liturgies like the Holy Eucharist, Morning Prayer, Evening Prayer, and Compline are the most-used services in the Episcopal Church. They are repeated again every week—if not every day in some communities—with a variation in the choice of hymns, scripture readings, and preaching. A good liturgy maintains the form, but allows great flexibility for the content to change. People do not seem to get tired of these forms, nor do they say, "I did the Eucharist once and that's all I need. I am in communion with God forever. I don't need it again." If we treat dialogue as a liturgy, we begin to see the value of repeated experiences of dialogue. Each time we do it, we learn more and gain more insights. By practicing the dialogue process regularly, the people in the multicultural community begin to see and experience the pattern with some regularity. In their repeated experience, a new context is built. In this new context, they feel a sense of consistency and safety, while at the same time their interest is kept up by the flexibility of content in the dialogue process.

In the five-session dialogue process described in Appendix B, each session begins with a process called "Conocimientos," followed by an opening prayer and dialogue ground rules. Mutual Invitation is used at least two to three times in each session. The session always ends with a prayer circle. These are the constant elements of the dialogue process. The differences among the sessions are the one or two activities addressing different facets of interracial issues. Every time the participants come together they know what to expect in terms of the overall format. This clarity of expectation creates safety and comfort. In that safety, participants are more open to examining their assumptions and listening to others who are different. By viewing dialogue as a liturgy, we provide safety for people to participate in the dialogue while teaching the participants to value dialogue as an ongoing, lifetime process.

Dialogue, like a liturgy, if repeated and modified over time according to the specific community, will become an form that is affirmed and owned by the whole community. When the multicultural community gathers, everyone will automatically act intentionally—"taking off their sandals"— as they enter the holy ground in which true dialogue can and will happen. The ground rules for dialogue become the covenant for communication in the community. Mutual Invitation becomes a "normal" process that we use for interaction. Dividing into small groups for discussion is perceived as a necessary process in order for the community to value cultural pluralism. When dialogue is repeated regularly like a liturgy, the interpathy and contextual evaluation skill level of the whole community increases. When the dialogue process becomes like a liturgy, it permeates the whole community; the opportunities for dialogue are everywhere: in meetings, Christian education classrooms, Bible study groups, youth gatherings, social ministry group meetings, the "coffee hour," Sunday morning liturgies, etc.

3. Liturgy is God-centered.

How does this repeated dialogue pattern differ from a ritual that we talked about as a golden calf in chapter 5? A ritual is a repeated pattern of behavior, but this pattern of behavior is often used to avoid dealing with the real issues. A person who goes through a ritual may think she or he is addressing the uncertainty in her or his life, but in actuality, it may or may not do that. A liturgy is different from a ritual because in its repeated pattern, it addresses the real issues in life by recognizing the presence of God. In a liturgy we listen to God, who gives us new insights into problems. With these new insights, we respond with courage to face our uncertainty. A ritual avoids the uncertainty; a liturgy helps us face it. A ritual runs around in circles, going nowhere; a liturgy spirals as it circles and moves us forward into constructive actions.

Dialogue has the danger of becoming a ritual that we use to avoid facing the real issues, if we don't treat it like a liturgy in which God is the center. When we repeat similar patterns of behavior, we may become too comfortable, and we may decide that we don't want to deal with anybody else who is not like us. We may build a golden calf and call it the dialogue process, and as long as we are circling around this golden calf, we believe that we are culturally sensitive people. We may build a new tower of Babel. We sit on top of the tower called dialogue and judge and exclude everyone else who does not talk or behave like us. When that happens, dialogue becomes an instrument of exclusion; it ceases to be holy and prophetic.

I have had extensive experience in facilitating dialogue sessions with both secular groups and Christian groups. I could sense that there was a qualitative difference between the two. In a secular group, without the theological foundation for dialogue, we rely on social and professional principles as its justification. In civic groups, the justification can be the United States Constitution and the Bill of Rights. In professional groups, such as those comprised of teachers or health-care providers, the justification for dialogue appeals to the participants' professional ethics. In business groups, the appeal is often to monetary profit. These values are important to uphold when working with these groups, but they may make a weak foundation for dialogue. They do not safeguard dialogue as a prophetic challenge to the organization. Dialogue faces a greater danger of becoming a ritual that the organization goes through, but has little effect, because the organization has no intention to change as a result of the dialogue process. The dialogue process in these groups tends to stay at the awareness level. The willingness to participate is lower. Group members feel less secure. The resulting action tends to be less effective and does not address the heart of the issue.

In order for our dialogue to be prophetic, we must act deliberately to invite God to enter into the dialogue consistently. When we evoke and remind ourselves of our relationship with God, dialogue becomes a liturgy. By evoking the relationship—our covenant with God—we enter into dialogue not just to deal with a dispute or an argument that can be resolved with a quick compromise. When the dialogue process becomes a liturgy, we build a context not only with each other but also with God. God becomes a third party that helps us make decisions according to God's context, forcing us to see that our different cultural contexts are only relative to each other. The gospel values become the ground rules—the new covenant—within which we can respect each other as fellow sons and daughters of God. When there is a theological foundation to dialogue, people are more willing to participate. People are more secure when they know dialogue is not just a ritual, but a liturgy in which God is there to heal us when we are hurt, judge us when we get scared and want to build a golden calf of avoidance, and help us to achieve reconciliation when we discover our sinfulness.

When the dialogue process becomes a liturgy, we have the potential to move the participants beyond mutual understanding and toward reconciliation, and communion with each other and with God. When the dialogue process becomes a liturgy, we are refined and purified each time we participate in the process, renewing our covenant with each other and with God. When the dialogue process becomes a liturgy, God invites us to trust God in the process, so that we can be safe and secure as we prophesy to each other. When the dialogue process becomes a liturgy, God takes the lead in the process to guide and support us out into the world to do the work of justice. When the dialogue process becomes a liturgy, the communities that engage in this process become a collective burning bush, shining brightly in a world darkened by destructive responses to intercultural issues.

CHAPTER THIRTEEN

Liturgy as Dialogue

In my ministry, people often ask me, "If you do an intercultural dialogue process like a liturgy, does that mean all liturgies are intercultural dialogue processes?"

"Not necessarily so," I answer. "Just as dialogue can fall into the danger of becoming a ritual that avoids, rather than addresses the real issues, liturgy also has the danger of becoming a ritual that avoids dealing with people who are different by excluding them."

"Then how do we design a liturgy for a multicultural community?" they ask. My response to this question is that in order for a liturgy to nurture and support a multicultural community, it needs the help of the dialogue process.

> The LORD said to Moses: Take sweet spices, stacte, and onycha, and galbanum, sweet spices with pure frankincense (an equal part of each), and make an incense blended as by the perfumer, seasoned with salt, pure and holy; and you shall beat some of it into powder, and put part of it before the covenant in the tent of meeting where I shall meet with you; it shall be for you most holy. When you make incense according to this composition, you shall not make it for yourselves; it shall be regarded by you as holy to the LORD. Whoever makes any like it to use as perfume shall be cut off from the people.
>
> Exodus 30:34–38

The admonition that "you shall not make it for yourselves" is clear and strong. "Whoever makes any like it to use as perfume shall be cut off from the people." We must not forget that a liturgy is done for God. The moment we make it into something that is for our own gain, we have turned the liturgy into a ritual, a golden calf of adultery. A liturgy can never be used as a "perfume" to cover up the real issues in our lives. Yet, very often, in the way many churches worship, a liturgy becomes a self-serving ritual that we use to make ourselves feel better and more secure while excluding anyone who does not know our "style of worship." In order to create a multicultural liturgy that does not exclude, liturgy needs the help of the dialogue process in two ways. First, liturgy needs the intercultural dialogue process to move between high- and low-context levels of participation. Second, liturgy needs the intercultural dialogue process to be prophetic.

1. Liturgy needs the intercultural dialogue process to move between high- and low-context levels of participation.

Our local church liturgies tend to be high context in the sense that people share a great deal of common understanding of what each symbol and action means in the liturgy. If the congregation has many longtime members, their knowledge of a common tradition would reinforce the high-context style of our liturgy even more. The confirmation class or new-member classes are places where we pre-program newcomers and children to share this context. Sometimes, when we repeat the same actions for so long, they become almost second nature. We forget that what we do in our liturgy is unique to us and our culture only, and proceed to assume that everyone should behave as we do when they come to worship with us—the gesture that we make when we enter the church, the way we sing our hymns, the way the sermon is done, and so on. Our liturgy can become very high-context, and that may unconsciously exclude anyone who did not have the pre-programming and therefore does not understand the meaning and values behind each element and action in the liturgy.

In a multicultural community, we no longer have the luxury to assume our members have a shared context. If we are an effective and growing community, there will be newcomers flowing in constantly every time we gather as a community. If we maintain our high-context style of communicating and worship, we will exclude these newcomers who do not share our context. Therefore, in order for a multicultural community to be continuously inclusive, we need to make our liturgy more like a dialogue process. A multicultural liturgy must begin as a low-context activity, giving explicit instructions about what is expected from the congregation in terms of behavior, and the rationale behind these behaviors. Obviously we cannot explain everything each time; that would be very cumbersome. But some kind of explanation on some of the major actions of the liturgy is crucial in the development of a multicultural community. The sermon is another low-context way of explaining our theology, our values, and beliefs. As the liturgy moves on, it has to move more and more toward the high-context side. The worship experience is most powerful when we move beyond the thinking and analytical (low-context) and are able to worship in a wholistic way in which meaning and action are one (high-context). Take the Eucharist as an example: The liturgy of the Word is a low-context way of building this common context. By the time we approach the table for communion, instead of thinking and explaining what it means to receive communion, we feel it, we experience it without the barrier of words. The context I share with the people around me at the communion table and the context I share with Christ and all the saints come together to provide this uplifting spiritual experience that can be accomplished only through a high-context process.

2. Liturgy needs intercultural dialogue to stay prophetic.

Each cultural group has a tendency to believe that its way of relating to God is the true and right way. Our liturgy may become a golden calf that gives us the same message again and again, making us feel safe and protected as long as we are doing the same liturgy. When we see another cultural group responding to God's call differently, we may judge them as not being faithful or not being real Christians. In order for such a community to stop playing God themselves and return to God, a prophetic voice needs to challenge this community. The prophetic voice can come from an individual or a group of people who, with God's direction, act deliberately to challenge the core assumptions of the community. Saints and prophets in centuries past have served in this role of acting apart from their cultures. In their deliberate acts, which are often contrary to the convention of their own cultural values, the presence of God is made known. The divine judgment is pronounced and the community recognizes its sinfulness. The covenant is renewed and their faith in God is restored.

If we incorporate the dialogue process in our liturgy by inviting different cultural groups into our midst, the different cultural groups become the prophetic voices for each other. If, in our liturgy, we invite people to engage in a dialogue process, sharing how different cultural groups interact with God differently, we acknowledge God's values as something that stands apart from any culture. In our dialogue, we realize that no one culture has exactly the same values as God's culture. We hear the prophetic voice in the midst of the dialogue process calling us to return to an ethnorelative vision of God.

> The fire on the altar shall be kept burning; it shall not go out. Every morning the priest shall add wood to it, lay out the burnt offering on it, and turn into smoke the fat pieces of the offerings of well-being. A perpetual fire shall be kept burning on the altar; it shall not go out.
>
> Leviticus 6:12–13

Liturgy in a multicultural community must keep the holy fire burning. It must not become a golden calf of avoidance and exclusion. To keep the fire burning, we must add wood to the holy fire every time we gather to do a liturgy. The wood is the recognition that there are people who are different in our midst. Their new perspectives are valued as much as those perspectives that we have had so far because they are the new wood that keeps the fire burning. If we do not add more wood, the fire will go out.

What are the key principles to bear in mind when we design a multicultural liturgy? How can we add wood to the fire to keep it going?

1. Make the instructional time a part of the liturgy.

In a multicultural community, we do not assume that everybody shares the same context. Therefore, our liturgy must begin in a low-context way, like a dialogue process, giving explicit behavioral instructions to everyone regarding the actions and meaning of the liturgy. This instructional time might seem very boring to those who already know them, but each liturgy is a sacrifice of new offering. In a multicultural liturgy, we sacrifice our familiarity with the liturgy and start anew, knowing that later on in the liturgy we will reach the point where we can worship with ease again. The first principle for designing a multicultural liturgy is to make the instructional time a part of the liturgy.

2. Use repetition to quickly build the shared context.

In a multicultural liturgy, inevitably, we would be asking participants to learn something new such as a song in another language, a dance from another tradition, or a custom from another culture. We must ensure that the new piece we ask the participants to do is something that is learnable in a short time within the liturgy. It would be even better if the new piece could be repeated within the same liturgy so that the comfort level of doing it will increase. When something is repeated over time, it becomes part of the shared context of the group.

For example, when I teach a congregation a new song, I do not assume that everyone in the congregation has the same musical skills. Therefore, the old way of announcing a hymn number and expecting people to read the music and learn to sing a new hymn consists of too many new elements to learn in such a short time. The old way assumes that everyone can read music, thereby excluding from participating those who do not know the hymn or who are unable to read music. In order to make learning a new song an empowering experience for everyone, I usually choose a short song. I invite people to listen to the whole song once. Then I invite them to repeat each phrase after me. Then the congregation is invited to sing the whole song, putting all the phrases together. Usually after about three tries, everyone in the congregation has learned the song, and with a few repetitions, they enter into a high-context way of singing by internalizing the song, feeling its meaning as they repeat the musical phrases. I can teach people to sing in any language with this method. (See Appendix E for a full description of this teaching process.) This method of teaching a congregation to sing is a real example of how to move people from a low-context state (the learning phase) to a high-context mode (internalizing the song) of worship using the technique of repetition.

This method is also useful in teaching the congregation new collective prayers. For most congregations, there are only a few shared prayers such as the Lord's Prayer. By teaching them more collective prayers using this method, we can increase the shared context of the congregation. Repetition is also a useful technique to help participants to reflect on the scriptural reading. Instead of reading three different passages and trying to preach on all three, I use one passage and read it two or three times. After each hearing of the passage, the congregation is invited to reflect on a specific question.

3. Keep the liturgy simple.

The number one mistake people make in planning a multicultural liturgy is that they try to do too much. "We ended up doing just about one of everything from every culture," they lament. By the time the congregation learns one thing, they have to move on to learn something else. This can be very unsettling. The liturgy becomes a struggle to learn all these new things, and the participants remain at the low-context learning mode, thereby never getting a chance to move into a high-context mode of worship. For example, the scriptural reading is often too long. By the time it is read in the various languages, it becomes too cumbersome. When I was at the TaizÈ community in France, I was amazed at how the liturgy can be done in five languages. One technique is to use short pieces that can be repeated many times over a short period of time. This technique is used for their music, prayers, and scriptural reading. The scriptural reading is very short; it can be read in five languages in less than three minutes. Instead of singing songs with many verses, they use songs with one very short phrase that can be repeated like a chant. To use an old proverb to express this principle: to learn a few things well is better than learning many things poorly.

A good principle to remember is that teaching the new material should be concentrated toward the beginning of the service. This new material should become more and more familiar to the congregation as the service moves on. This might mean repeating the new material in appropriate places. Toward the second half of the service, everything should be familiar to the congregation so that its members can worship in the high-context mode.

4. Commit oneself to cultural pluralism.

In order to maintain our commitment of cultural pluralism, a multicultural liturgy must include and welcome different cultural perspectives. We must convey to the congregation that unity does not mean sameness. We must help them appreciate the validity of each culture's different ways of relating to God, even though they may not understand them fully. Part of the essence of a liturgy is the mystery that it presents to us. We understand God, yet do not fully comprehend. Our commitment to cultural pluralism is another way of affirming this mystery. For example, when I am invited to preach in a bilingual/bicultural congregation, I prepare two different sermons—one in each language. Because the two cultural groups have two different contexts, the theological reflection has to be different, since God challenges and affirms each culture differently. Only the bilingual people in the congregation will discover that the two sermons are not the same. But if they are forewarned, they may even pay more attention to what is being said. Furthermore, I give an "assignment" for the groups when the sermon is given in the language that they do not understand. For example, before I preach in Chinese, I invite the English-speaking members of the congregation to read the Bible passage for the day a couple of times and reflect on a specific question that I give them. Then I proceed to preach in Chinese. After I preach in Chinese, I instruct the Chinese-speaking members to reflect on a specific question that I give them while I preach in English. This is a practical way of affirming cultural pluralism in the liturgy. By releasing the need to understand everything in the liturgy, the participants can be free to use the time for their own reflection and growth. Instead of worrying about what is being said in a language they do not understand, they use the time productively and spiritually.

Another way to uphold our commitment to cultural pluralism is to invite people from different cultural perspectives to share their reflections on the same scriptural passage. This can be done sequentially, as in a panel of speakers, or it can be done in small-group dialogue. Instead of a sermon, I have done liturgies in which the sermon time is used for small-group sharing. (See Appendix A for using small group biblical reflection in a multicultural liturgy.) In the dialogue process, we present and affirm that God works through each culture differently. As we hear how the gospel story connects with the different cultural stories, our perception of God is expanded beyond our own ethnocentrism. When our liturgy, like a dialogue process, commits to cultural pluralism, it maintains the tension between the different cultural perspectives. We assure the community that we can disagree and still be in the same community, worshiping the same God. In our prayers, we ask God to help us with our struggle to listen to each other. We ask God to give us strength to hold on to two seemingly opposing perspectives without breaking off. We ask God to affirm our spirituality of creative marginality, like God affirmed Abraham, Moses, the prophets, St. Paul, and all the saints.

Liturgy is the center of a community. It holds the community of faith together. When we commit ourselves to developing a multicultural community, our liturgy must also be our center. Our liturgy must also become a dialogue process that calls forth people to come down from their towers of ethnocentrism and experience God in a ethnorelative way. Our liturgy must light the holy fire that draws us together in the wilderness. Our liturgy must nurture us when we are disappointed and frustrated as we wander in the wilderness of racial intolerance. Our liturgy must challenge us when we get scared and want to build a golden calf. Our liturgy must continually remind us to enter the dialogue process with each other and with God, renewing our covenant again and again. Our liturgy must become a holy fire of purification. Our liturgy must be the holy ground on which the burning bush will blaze, but not consume.

> The fire on the altar shall be kept burning; it shall not go out.
>
> Leviticus 6:12

Appendix A

An Intercultural Dialogue/
Worship Service

Concerning the Service:

This is a three-hour liturgy designed in the structure of the Holy Eucharist. The Celebrant is the minister presiding over the service, especially at the communion table. The Dialogue Coordinator is the one who oversees the dialogue process within the service.

To prepare for this service, the dialogue coordinator has to recruit the appropriate number of facilitators who can facilitate the following three sections of the service:

1. Biblical Reflection Process
2. Intragroup Dialogue Process
3. Intergroup Dialogue Process

Material required for this service:

1. flip-chart paper
2. markers
3. masking tape
4. copies of the Litany for Dialogue

This service can also be used as an inauguration of a longer dialogue program similar to the one described in Appendix B.

+ + + + +

Gather in Christ's Name

A hymn, psalm, or anthem may be sung.

The Celebrant greets the people, saying:

Dear brothers and sisters in Christ: We gather here at this time and place to pray and to dialogue with each other about our commonalities and differences. Throughout the history of the church, conflict among members of the body of Christ is common and sometimes inevitable: conflict among Jesus' disciples, disputes between Peter and Paul, controversy over whether Gentiles can be Christians, and disagreement about which book to include in the Christian Scriptures, just to name a few. They are part of what it means to live in any diverse community. As Christians, we have Jesus Christ, our great mediator and reconciler, who teaches us to love our neighbor as ourselves and to love our enemies. If we commit ourselves to the dialogue and reconciliation process, we will discover the full meaning of living in Christ's community where truth and justice can be found for all.

A Litany for Dialogue[1]

A leader may lead the litany for dialogue. The people respond to each petition with "Hear our prayer."
Let us pray:

O God, you made us in your own image: with eyes to see, ears to listen, mouths to speak, and hearts to feel, and through Jesus, you have shown us how to see and perceive, listen and discern, speak and illuminate, and feel and be moved with compassion:

Help us to realize that we are not here to debate who is right and who is wrong, but to experience true dialogue in which we strive to communicate honestly and listen actively and openly to each other.

God, in your mercy,
Hear our prayer.

Give us the wisdom to recognize our preconceived assumptions and perceptions about others—some are conscious; some are unconscious. Make us aware of how our assumptions influence the way we listen and interpret others' words and actions, and how they affect the way we speak and act in the group.

God, in your mercy,
Hear our prayer.

---

[1] A similar version of the Litany for Dialogue appeared in Kittredge Cherry & Zalmon Sherwood, eds. *Equal Rites* (Louisville: Westminster John Knox Press, 1995), pp. 32–33.

Open our hearts and minds to experience new ideas, feelings, situations, and people even though, at times, we may feel awkward and uncomfortable.

God, in your mercy,
Hear our prayer.

Give us the strength to take responsibility for what we say and what we say on behalf of our group. Equip our tongues with eloquence so to reveal the truth of our lives and our communities so that others can hear and understand.

God, in your mercy,
Hear our prayer.

Expand our listening ability to include not just the words we hear, but also feelings, body language, and varieties of silence that humankind uses to communicate.

God, in your mercy,
Hear our prayer.

Give us the courage to take responsibility for our own feelings as they surface and help us find ways to express them without blaming others so that we can hear and learn constructively the consequences of each other's words and actions.

God, in your mercy,
Hear our prayer.

Keep us under the shadow of your wings and make this place a sanctuary in which we will respect each other by holding the personal information shared here in confidence, because only in your love can we feel free to say what is in our minds and hearts.

God, in your mercy,
Hear our prayer.

The celebrant concludes:

O God, as we enter your sanctuary of grace and reconciliation, take away the arrogance and hatred that infect our hearts; break down the walls that separate us; unite us in bonds of love; and work through our struggle and confusion to accomplish your purposes on earth; that, in your good time, all people may serve you in harmony as one body; through Jesus Christ, our great reconciler and mediator.

Amen.

Proclaim the Word of God

The following lesson or another appropriate lesson is read.

Acts 2: 1–13 (Pentecost)

Other lessons that may be appropriate for this service:
Genesis 11:1–9 (The Tower of Babel)
Isaiah 11:6–9 (The Peaceable Kingdom)
Ezekiel 36:22–28 (A New Heart I'll Give to You)
1 Corinthians 4:1–5 (No Passing Premature Judgment)
1 Corinthians 12:12–13 (14–21) 22–26 (27–30) (Body
of Christ)
Luke 6:20–26 (The Beatitudes)
Matthew 5:43–48 (Love Your Enemies)
Matthew 7:1–5 (Do Not Judge)

Biblical Reflection Process

(Total time required for a group of eight: 45 minutes.)

1. Divide into small groups of six to eight persons making sure that each group has a facilitator.

2. The facilitator explains the Mutual Invitation process.

3. Using the Mutual Invitation process, invite each person in the group to share:

A word or a phrase that stands out for you.

4. Invite someone within the small group to read the passage again.

5. Again using Mutual Invitation, invite each person to answer the following questions. (These questions are specifically for Acts 2:1–13. If another lesson is used, determine an appropriate question ahead of time and give it to the facilitators.)

Is this a miracle of the tongue or is this a miracle of the ear? What has been your experience?

6. Invite someone within the small group to read the passage again.

7. Again using Mutual Invitation, invite each person to answer the following question:

For the purpose of our day together, what does God invite you to do through this passage today?

8. The facilitator writes down on chart paper the answers to the last question and then posts it on the wall.

Intercultural Dialogue as a Response to God's Word.

(Total time required: 1.5 hours)

A hymn may be sung to gather the congregation.

The Dialogue Coordinator may say:

The purpose of this gathering is to bring together people from diverse ethnic and cultural backgrounds to engage in dialogue with each other in the context of our worship. True dialogue is a conversation on a common subject between two or more persons of differing views. The primary purpose of dialogue is for each person to learn from the other so that he or she can change and grow. We believe our commitment to dialogue with each other will effect constructive change in race relations within the church and in the communities in which we reside.

As a continuation of our response to God's word, we invite you to go into different group formations for dialogue. The first groups we invite you to form are self-selected "cultural" groups. For some of us the choice might be obvious; for others, it may require some thinking. A cultural group can be formed based on race or ethnicity, gender, sexual orientation, physical ability, age, language, place of origin, and others. The purpose for forming groups in this way is to give members of each cultural group a chance to share and discuss what it means to be a part of that cultural group in the United States. We believe that the intercultural dialogue process, in which we will engage later this afternoon, will be more fruitful if each person enters it with a clearer sense of his or her cultural identity. In your group, a facilitator will give you instructions and questions to be discussed.

Intragroup Dialogue

Facilitators will help participants discern what group to join. Each group will have a facilitator who can identify with that particular "cultural" group:

1. *Divide into self-selected "cultural" groups*
2. *Invite participants to discuss the following:*
   a. *What is the history of my group in the United States?*
   b. *List at least three contributions.*
   c. *List at least three struggles.*
3. *The facilitator records the contributions and struggles on chart paper and then posts it.*

4. Each group reports to the whole congregation the result of their sharing, using their wall chart.

After each group has had a chance to report, the Dialogue Coordinator may say:

I now invite you to take a moment of silence to reflect on what you have heard. What did you feel as the different groups were reporting? *(pause)* Why did you feel that way? *(pause)* Take out a piece of paper and complete the following sentences:

I heard _____.

I feel _____.

One thing on which I need clarification is _____

_____.

Give the congregation a few minutes of silence to complete the sentences.

I now invite you to form mixed cultural groups of six to eight people. Your group should have a balance of members from all the different cultural groups. In your group, you will share the completed sentences using Mutual Invitation. After each person has shared, you can answer each other's clarification questions. There will be a facilitator in each group to give you further instruction.

Intergroup Dialogue

Facilitators will help participants break into groups. Once the group is formed, follow the process below:

1. Review the Litany for Dialogue recited at the beginning of the service. (Make sure the participants have copies of the litany.)

2. Invite participants to reaffirm what was said in the litany.

3. Introduce the Mutual Invitation process, again emphasizing the "pass" rule.

4. Invite participants to share their completed sentences without discussion. The facilitator writes the clarification questions on chart paper.

5. After everyone has had a chance to share, the facilitator invites the participants to help each other answer the clarification questions.

Prayers of the People

Staying in the small group, the facilitator may say:

Thank you all for sharing. Let us conclude the dialogue portion of the service by entering into prayer. I invite you to spend a moment thinking about how to complete the following sentences:

I thank God today _____.

I ask God today _____.

Allow a period of silence. The facilitator continues:

Let's join hands in a circle. I will start by sharing, "I thank God today...and I ask God today...." After I am done, I will squeeze the hand of the person on my right. That will be the signal for him/her to offer his/her prayer. When she finishes, she then squeezes the hand of the person on her right. If you don't want to say anything, just pass the pulse to the next person. When the pulse comes back to me, I will start saying the Lord's Prayer and I invite you to join me.

After each circle has recited the Lord's Prayer, a hymn may be sung to gather the congregation.

If this service is used as an inauguration of a longer dialogue program like the one described in Appendix B, the Dialogue Coordinator invites congregation members to sign up for a follow-up dialogue group.

The celebrant concludes this time of dialogue and prayer with the following prayer of thanksgiving or some other suitable prayer.

O God, who created all peoples in your image, we thank you for the wonderful diversity of races and cultures in this world. Enrich our lives by ever-widening circles of fellowship, and show us your presence in those who differ most from us, until our knowledge of your love is made perfect in our love for all your children; through Jesus Christ our Lord.[2]

Amen.

---

[2] This prayer is found on p. 840 of the 1979 *Book of Common Prayer* of the Episcopal Church.

The Peace

The celebrant may say to the people

> The peace of the Lord be always with you.

People **And also with you.**

All greet one another in the name of the Lord.

When communion is not to follow, the service concludes here.

Prepare the Table

Some of those present prepare the table; the bread, the cup of wine, and other offerings, are placed upon it. If congregation members have signed up for follow-up dialogue groups, the lists can be part of the offering.

Make Eucharist

The celebrant praises God for the salvation of the world through Jesus Christ. The celebrant then consecrates the bread and the cup using words instituted by Jesus at the Last Supper.

Break the Bread

Share the Gifts of God

The service concludes with a prayer of thanksgiving, and a dismissal

> Let us go forth into the world, rejoicing in the
> power of the Spirit.

People **Thanks be to God**.

Appendix B

A Five-Session Intercultural Dialogue Program

Concerning the Dialogue Program:

This is a five-session dialogue program in which each session builds on the last one. It is essential that all the participants are committed to attend all five sessions.

Each session has the same structure. The reason behind this consistent format is that it will provide the participants with a clear expectation for each session and they will feel more secure as they gain more familiarity with the format. The ideal size of the group should be ten to fifteen people.

In general, the material that you will need for each session includes:

name tags	masking tape
flip-chart	watercolor markers
chart paper	writing paper

(Material needed for a specific session will be listed.)

Each session lasts for two hours. An approximate time required for each portion of the process is provided. These time estimates are but guideposts as you facilitate the session.

The requirement for the dialogue space is that it be a large, bright room with a blank wall for putting up charts. There should be movable chairs for everyone in the group.

To reduce anxiety for the participants, post signs outside indicating the location of the dialogue session.

Session One

GOALS:
To introduce the participants to the dialogue process.
To introduce participants to each other.
To share experiences of being different.

ADDITIONAL MATERIAL FOR THIS SESSION:
Handout: Communication Ground Rules (Use Figure 10.1 in chapter 10.)

135

PREPARATION:

Conocimientos Chart

Before participants arrive, tape together chart paper to form a long chart on which you can put the following topics across the top: (See Diagram 1.)

NAME

MEANING OF YOUR NAME

BIRTHPLACE

YOUR GRANDPARENTS' BIRTHPLACES

ONE VALUE YOU LEARNED FROM YOUR
            PARENTS THAT YOU WILL PASS ON TO
            FUTURE GENERATIONS

ONE THING YOU WILL NOT PASS ON

Arrange chairs in a semicircle around the chart.

As participants arrive, give them name tags and invite them to fill in the columns on the chart.

PROCESS:

I. *Opening Prayer* (1 minute)

The facilitator may read the following opening prayer or some other suitable prayer:

Let us begin our meeting with a prayer. Let us pray:

O God, you made us in your own image and redeemed us through Jesus your Son: Look with compassion on the whole human family; take away the arrogance and hatred which infect our hearts; break down the walls that separate us; unite us in bonds of love; and work through our struggle and confusion to accomplish your purposes on earth; that, in your good time, all nations and races may serve you in harmony around your heavenly throne; through Jesus Christ our Lord.[1] *Amen.*

II. *Purpose of Gathering* (1 minute)

The facilitator continues by reading the following purpose statement of the gathering:

---

[1]This prayer is found on p. 815 of the 1997 *Book of Common Prayers* of the Episcopal Church.

DIAGRAM 1 — CONOCIMIENTOS CHART

NAME	MEANING OF YOUR NAME	BIRTH-PLACE	YOUR GRANDPARENTS' BIRTHPLACES	ONE VALUE THAT YOU LEARNED FROM YOUR PARENTS THAT YOU'LL PASS ON TO THE NEXT GENERATION	ONE THING THAT YOU WILL NOT PASS ON TO THE NEXT GENERATION
1					
2					
3					
4					
5					
6					
7					
8					
9					
10					
11					
12					
13					
14					
15					
16					
17					
18					
19					
20					

(General Purpose)

Welcome to the Intercultural Dialogue program. The purpose of these gatherings is to bring together people from diverse ethnic and cultural backgrounds to engage in dialogue with each other. True dialogue is a conversation on a common subject between two or more persons of differing views. The primary purpose of dialogue is for each person to learn from the other so that he or she can change and grow. We believe our commitment to dialogue with each other will effect constructive change in race relations within the church and in the communities in which we reside.

(Purpose for this session)

In the five sessions, we will have opportunities to share our own values, beliefs, and experiences; we will address issues such as stereotype, discrimination, racism, and institutional exclusion. Finally, we will explore ways to address intercultural issues for our own community. In the next two hours, we will introduce ourselves to each other, begin to look at the values that we hold, and share our experiences of being different.

III.   *Ground Rules* (10 minutes)

Hand out copies of Communication Ground Rules. *Give the following explanation:*

We, people from different cultural backgrounds, bring with us different assumptions of communication styles. Sometimes, these different assumptions will cause conflict and communication breakdown. Therefore, before we begin our dialogue together, we must first state the common ground rules that we all can agree upon. I will read them now.

After reading, ask participants if there are questions. Discuss the Communication Ground Rules *briefly.*

IV.   *Conocimientos* [2] (40 minutes)

Give the following instructions for the introductory process:

In order to help us get to know each other better, I invite you to

---

[2]This exercise is adapted from "Quienes Somos" by Francisco M. Hernandez, Talleres del Valle, 1974. The National Conference, Los Angeles Region has used this process extensively in its dialogue programs.

introduce yourselves using a process called "Conocimientos." The chart you filled out on the wall when you arrived was only the beginning of the process. I, as your facilitator, will begin by introducing myself using the categories on the Conocimientos chart. After I have finished, I will invite another person to introduce himself or herself. After that person finishes, that person is given the privilege to invite the next person. We will do this until everyone in the group has been invited. We have set aside about 30 minutes for this process. That means each person will have ____ minutes to share. I will ask you to respect other people's time as you share. Are there any questions?

The facilitator then begins the process by introducing himself/ herself.

When everyone has introduced himself or herself, the facilitator debriefs the group by asking the following questions:

What did you learn from this process?
In what way did the process help you understand each other?
Was there anything that you heard that surprised you?
What are some of the things we have in common?
What are the differences?

V.   *10-Minute Break*

VI.   *Mutual Invitation* (3 minutes)

Rearrange the chairs in a circle and invite participants to sit down. Give the following instruction:

Let's continue our dialogue process. In the Conocimientos process, we used an invitation format to invite each other to share. This is part of a process called "Mutual Invitation" we have used very effectively for a multicultural group. I will describe this process again so that everyone will know how we will proceed from here.

In order to ensure that everyone who wants to share has the opportunity to speak, we will proceed in the following way:

> A facilitator or a designated person will share first. After that person has spoken, he or she then invites another to share. The person you invite does not need to be the person next to you. After the next person has spoken, that

person is given the privilege to invite another to share. If you don't want to say anything, simply say "pass" and proceed to invite another to share. We will do this until everyone has been invited.

We will use this method of sharing at least two more times. After that, we can open the floor for general discussion. Are there any questions about the process?

VII.   *Times When We Felt "Different"* [3] (40 minutes)

Introduce the topic of sharing this way:

Consider a time in your childhood and a time in your adulthood when you realized you were "different." The difference could be your gender, race, class, religion, language, etc. I invite you to spend five minutes drawing pictures depicting the memory–one picture for the childhood experience, one picture for the adult experience—or, if you prefer, you may write and describe it. Please do this in silence. You might want to represent these experiences literally or symbolically. We are not looking for artistic ability here, but insight and honesty.

After participants have completed the picture, the facilitator gives the following instruction:

I invite you to share using Mutual Invitation. After one round of Mutual Invitation, we can open the floor for general discussion. Are there any questions about the process?

The facilitator begins the process by sharing his or her pictures.

VIII.   *Reflection on the Experience* (10 minutes)

The facilitator repeats the goals of the session and then helps the group reflect on the experience by asking the following questions:

How did you feel about today's session?
What did you learn?
How can we as a group improve our communication with each other?

---

[3]This process was originally designed by Lucky Altman. It is used widely in the Interracial Dialogue Series and numerous workplace diversity programs of the National Conference, Los Angeles Region.

The facilitator writes down the learnings and future improvements on the flip-chart.

IX. *Closing Prayer* (5 minutes)

The facilitator closes the meeting by saying the following:

Thank you all for sharing. I look forward to learning more at our next meeting. To close our time together, I invite you to spend a moment thinking about how to complete the following sentences:

I thank God today…
I ask God today…

Allow a period of silence. The facilitator continues:

Let's join hands in a circle. I will start by sharing my prayer, "I thank God today, and I ask God today…." After I am finished, I will squeeze the hand of the person on my right. That will be the signal for him or her to offer his or her prayer. When she or he finishes, she or he then squeezes the hand of the person on the right. If you don't want to say anything, just pass the pulse to the next person. When the pulse comes back to me, I will start saying the Lord's Prayer and I invite you to join me.

Session Two

GOALS:
To share racial/cultural identities and to examine assumptions and preconceptions we have about different groups.

ADDITIONAL MATERIAL FOR THIS SESSION:
Work sheets for Origins of Images

PREPARATION:
Conocimientos Chart
Before participants arrive, extend the Conocimientos chart with additional chart paper and put the following topics across the top:

— **How would you identify yourself culturally?**

— **Name one advantage of having this identity.**

— **Name one issue you face by having this identity.**

Arrange chairs in a semicircle around the Conocimientos chart.

Create two other charts with the following information:
Chart #1

> List: **Korean American, African American, European American, Armenian, Soviet immigrant, Mexican national, Mexican American, Central American, Chinese American, Iranian, Gay and Lesbian... etc.**

Chart #2

> F = ideas received from family of origin
> P = personal or professional interaction
> M = media
> E = education

As participants arrive, give them name tags and invite them to fill in the added columns on the Conocimientos chart.

PROCESS:

   I. *Opening Prayer* (1 minute)
       (See Session One.)

   II. *Purpose of the Gathering* (1 minute)
       (See Session One for General Purpose.)

In the next two hours, we will share with each other our racial/cultural identities and examine assumptions and preconceptions we have about different groups.

   III. *Ground Rules* (10 minutes)
       (See Session One.)

   IV. *Conocimientos* (40 minutes)
       (See Session One.)

   V. *Origins of Images* [4] (40 minutes)

Hand out the work sheets. Explain the process in the following way:

---

[4]This process was also originally designed by Lucky Altman and is used widely in the Interracial Dialogue Series and various workplace diversity programs of the National Conference, Los Angeles Region.

The next process is called "Origins of Images." This exercise helps us examine the images we hold in our minds about the "others" with whom we may or may not have personal contact. In your work sheets, there are four quadrants. In each quadrant, you may fill in the name of an ethnic or cultural group other than yours. Here are some examples.

Point to Chart #1.

The facilitator may want to give participants two headings that everyone should have and then give them a choice for the other two. Give participants time to fill in the headings.

Now, I invite you to write down all the words or phrases that come to mind about the "groups" listed on the work sheet. Do not judge what comes to your mind. Simply write it down. This is for your own reflection and will not be collected.

Give participants time to write.

Now, next to each word or phrase, *(point to Chart #2)* write the letter F for ideas received from family of origin, P for ideas from personal or professional interaction, M for media, and E for education.

Again, give participants time to do this.

I invite you to share what you have learned from completing the work sheet using the Mutual Invitation process. If you don't want to share anything, you can pass.

After each participant has had a chance to share, the facilitator opens the floor for general discussion.

VI. *Reflection on the Experience* (10 minutes)
    (See Session One.)

VII. *Closing Prayer* (5 minutes)
    (See Session One.)

Session Three

GOALS:
To examine and confront the issues of prejudice, discrimination, and racism, and how they affect us personally.

ADDITIONAL MATERIAL FOR THIS SESSION:
Photolanguage: "Interactions" [5]

PREPARATION:
                    Conocimientos Chart:
Before participants arrive, extend the chart with additional paper
and write the following topics across the top:

— **What comes to mind when you hear the words** *prejudice,*
   discrimination?

Chart for Photolanguage:
     Answer
                    What is racism?
        and/or
                    How has racism affected your life?
        and/or
                    What is it like being a victim of racism?
     in 1, 2, or 3 photos.

As participants arrive, give them name tags and invite them to fill
in the added column on the Conocimientos chart.

PROCESS:

  I.   *Opening Reflection* (1 minute)
       (See Session One.)

  II. *Purpose of the Gathering* (1 minute)
       (See Session One for General Purpose.)

In the next two hours, we will examine and confront the issues of
prejudice, discrimination, and racism and how they affect us
personally.

  III. *Ground Rules* (3 minutes)
       (See Session One.)

  IV. *Conocimientos* (20 minutes)
       (See Session One.)

---

[5]*Interactions* is published by Inspiral Productions. You can purchase a
copy by writing: Inspiral Productions, 3175 S. Hoover Street, Box 357, Los
Angeles, CA 90007-3164.

Origins of Images Work Sheet

V.   *10-Minute Break*

VI.   *Photolanguage* (40 minutes)

Rearrange the chairs in a circle in one area of the room. In a separate area of the room, display all the photos on three large tables without crowding them. Make sure there is room around each table for participants to move around. If tables are not available, sometimes displaying the photos on the floor will do. The facilitator invites participants to sit down.

The facilitator describes the process for using Photolanguage according to instructions given in the packet. The instructions also can be found in Appendix B of The Wolf Shall Dwell with the Lamb. *The reflection questions are:*

Answer:

> **What is racism?**

and/or

> **How has racism affected your life?**

and/or

> **What is it like being a victim of racism?**

in 1, 2, or 3 photos.

After each participant has shared, the facilitator invites the group to further dialogue with the following instructions:

I invite you to look at all the selected photos again. Take out a piece of paper and spend five minutes writing down some thoughts and ideas on how we, as the church, can address the issue of racism.

Give participants time to write.

Again, using the Mutual Invitation process, I invite you to share some of your thoughts and ideas on how we, as the church, can address the issue of racism.

The facilitator takes notes on the flip-chart while the participants are sharing.

After everyone has shared, the facilitator opens the floor for discussion by asking the following questions:

Are there any clarifications that you want to ask of each other? Does anyone want to add anything to what he or she said?

VIII.   *Reflection on the Session* (10 minutes)

(See Session One.)

IX. *Closing Reflection* (5 minutes)
(See Session One.)

Session Four

GOALS:
To explore and understand institutional racism and how we can combat it.

ADDITIONAL MATERIAL FOR THIS SESSION:
Power Circle Reflection Sheets

PREPARATION:
Conocimientos Chart:
Before participants arrive, extend the chart with additional paper and write the following topic across the top:
> **One word to depict the feeling of being excluded.**
> **What does true inclusion mean?**

Arrange chairs in a semicircle around the chart.

As participants arrive, give them name tags and invite them to fill in the added column on the chart.

PROCESS:

I. **Opening Reflection** (1 minute)
   (See Session One.)

II. **Purpose of the Gathering** (1 minute)
   (See Session One for General Purpose.)

In the next two hours, we will explore together and try to understand better the issue of institutional racism and how we can combat it.

III. **Ground Rules** (3 minutes)
   (See Session One.)

IV. **Conocimientos** (20 minutes) (Optional)
   (See Session One.)

V. *Power Circle* (20 minutes)

Make sure the space in which the next exercise is done is free of sharp objects or furnishings that would injure participants during this physical process. Explain the process in the following way:

The next process I invite you to participate in involves physical movement and touching—mostly holding hands. If you are physically challenged, pregnant, or if you have strong feelings about touching and being touched, come talk to me and I will give you another role in this process. Now I invite you to stand up, move over there, and stand in a circle holding hands.

Give participants time to settle into the circle. Give those who opted out the role(s) of a timekeeper and/or an observer.

Now, imagine there is something inside the circle that you really want—something that you want to have, something that you want to protect. (*Pause*) Each one of you will take a turn being outside the circle. The person outside has one minute to get in the circle in any way possible. The circle is to try every strategy to keep the person out. Independent of whether or not you make it inside the circle, within the minute, you can rejoin the circle and invite the next person to be outside. Any questions?

When all the questions are answered, the facilitator invites the first participant to be out. Make sure you or someone is keeping time, and call out when one minute is over if the outsider did not get in. If the activity gets to be too violent, the facilitator should stop the exercise to remind people to be more careful.

After everyone has a turn, invite participants to go back to sitting in a circle. Hand out reflection sheets. Invite participants to complete the reflection sheets.

Give participants time to write.

Collect all the sheets and take a ten-minute break.

VI. *10-Minute Break*

During the break, the facilitator, observers, and others write down all the reflection sheet responses on separate pieces of chart paper— one chart per question.

VII.   *Debrief Power Circle*[6] (35 minutes)

Invite participants to sit down again. Use the following questions to debrief the Power Circle.

Let's look at the responses for the question: How did it feel to be outside the circle?

> Did you see any common themes in these responses? What are they?

In the institutions with which we interact, church, work place, school...etc., have you found yourself feeling this way?

Invite responses.

Now let's look at the responses for the question: What strategies did you use to get in the circle?
When we feel excluded from a group or an organization, have we used these strategies to get in? If you are comfortable with it, you may share some of these incidents with the group.

Invite responses.

Let's look at the responses for the question: What strategies did you use to keep people out?

> In the organizations, institutions, and groups that we belong to, how have we kept people out by using these strategies?
>
> What were you trying to protect?

Invite responses.

Now let's look at the responses for the question: How does it feel to be part of the circle that keeps people out?
As time went by, did your attitude change? How?

Invite responses.

If the observers have not given their input in the discussion, ask them to give feedback.

VIII.   *Reflection on the Session* (10 minutes)
   (See Session One.)

IX.   *Closing Prayer* (5 minutes)
   (See Session One.)

---

[6]A similar process can be found called "Circle Break-in" in Judy H. Katz, *White Awareness: Handbook for Anti-Racism Training* (Norman and London: University of Oklahoma Press, 1978), pp. 100–101.

Session Five

GOALS:
To explore ways to change individual and institutional behaviors and attitudes that will foster a more inclusive community.

PREPARATION:
Conocimientos Chart: (Optional)
Before participants arrive, extend the chart with additional paper and write the following topics across the top:

What comes to mind when you hear the word *difference*?`
What are the essential elements of an inclusive community?

Arrange chairs in a semicircle around the chart.

Create two charts with the following information.

Chart #1:
1. **My growth and change as a result of this dialogue program.**
2. **My next step.**

Chart #2:
1. **Where is my community now in dealing with intercultural issues?**
2. **What would be a positive step that my community could take? In what concrete ways can my community take this step?**

As participants arrive, give them name tags and invite them to fill in the added column on the chart.

PROCESS:

I.   *Opening Reflection* (1 minute)
(See Session One.)

II.   *Purpose of the Gathering* (1 minute)
(See Session One for General Purpose.)
In the next two hours, we will explore ways to change individual and institutional behaviors and attitudes that will foster a more inclusive community.

III.   *Ground Rules* (3 minutes)
(See Session One.)

IV.   *Conocimientos* (20 minutes) (Optional)
(See Session One.)

Power Circle Reflection Sheet

How did you feel about being outside the circle and trying to get in?

What strategies did you use to try to get in?

What strategies did the circle use to keep people out?

How did you feel about being part of the circle that kept people out?

V.   *Then and Now* (40 minutes)

The facilitator gives the following explanation of the next process:

The next process will help each one of us recapture our growth and change as a result of our dialogue together.

Read the following slowly and clearly with pauses in the appropriate places.

I invite you to close your eyes. Relax. I invite you to go back to the first day of the Intercultural Dialogue Program. Picture yourself clearly in your mind. You entered the room where the first session was held. What was your attitude toward this program? What was your attitude toward intercultural issues? What were your expectations? As I summarize some of the activities that we did throughout this program, I invite you to track your own growth and changes.

We began each session with a process called Conocimientos, which invited us to write down and discuss various topics at each session. We shared our experience of being different; we explored our cultural identities; we examined the origins of our images of other racial and ethnic groups; we dealt with racism using Photolanguage; we discussed the issue of inclusion and exclusion by role-playing the power circle. Spend a moment again to recapture your growth and change through these processes. *(Pause)* Who are you now as a result of our time together? Are there differences between who you are now and who you were before this program? *(Pause)* Consider the journey that you have taken through this dialogue program and look at the future now. What is your next step? What might you do to continue the process? *(Pause)* Now, I invite you to take out a piece of paper and write down your growth and change as a result of this program and your step. *(Refer to Chart #1)*

Give participants time to write.

Invite participants to share what they wrote using the Mutual Invitation Process.

The facilitator may record the sharing on the flip-chart.

VI.   *Taking the Learning Home* (20 minutes)

Invite participants to discuss the following questions:

(Refer to Chart #2)

1. Where is my community now in dealing with intercultural issues?

2. What would be a positive step that my community could take? In what concrete ways can my community take this step?

Write on the flip-chart the steps at which the group arrives.

VII. *Reflection on the Whole Dialogue Program* (15 minutes)

The facilitator helps the group reflect on the experience by asking the following questions:

How did you feel about this dialogue program?
What did you learn?
What was most helpful?
If we are to do it again, how can we improve it?

A facilitator writes on the flip-chart learning and future improvements.

VIII. *Closing Reflection* (5 minutes)
  (See Session One.)

A Dialogue Process: Focusing on Differences in Communication Styles

Concerning this Dialogue Process

This is a two-hour dialogue process. The facilitator should be familiar with Hall's concept of high- and low-context styles of communication.

You can expand this process into a three hour process by adding the Biblical Reflection Process using the Pentecost passage. (See Appendix A.)

GOALS:
To help participants gain a deeper understanding and assess their own communication style using the high/low-context continuum and to find concrete ways to improve their communication skills as individuals and as a community.

Type of Group: This is particularly effective for participants who are or will be working together in the same church or organization.

Size of Group: No more than 20

Setting: Large room in which participants can move around and form small groups.

Materials: Flip-chart, markers, masking tape.

Handouts:
1. Respectful Communication Guidelines (Figure 10.2 in chapter 10)
2. Characteristics of High- and Low-Context Communication Styles (Figure 11.1 in chapter 11)
3. Self-Assessment Work Sheet

PROCESS:

Step One:
Review and discuss Respectful Communication Guidelines.

Step Two:
Distribute the "Characteristics of High- and Low-Context Communication Styles" and the "Self-Assessment Work Sheet" handouts. Give a short presentation on the difference between high- and low-context communication styles. You can do this by reading excerpts from chapter 11. Invite participants to review the concepts and spend 5 minutes completing the Self-Assessment Work Sheet.

Step Three:
Divide the room into three areas and label them:
    High-Context
    Medium-Context
    Low-Context

Invite participants to move to the areas of the room according to their self-assessment on the high/low-context continuum: 1 and 2 will go to the low-context section; 3 and 4 will go to the medium-context section; 5 and 6 will go to the high-context section.

Step Four:
Invite participants to read aloud their self-observations that support their self-assessment. If they don't have one, they can pass.

Step Five:
After hearing the self-observations of each group, participants may choose to move to a different group. *(Reason: They may have gotten a clearer understanding of the concept and are able to make a more accurate self-assessment.)*

Step Six:
Give each group flip-chart paper and markers. Invite them to write down on the paper their responses to the last question of the work sheet.

Step Seven:
Invite the groups to display their charts and give a short report. Participants can ask clarification questions and give feedback after each report. For example, after a report from the low-context group, the high-context group can respond by giving feedback regarding whether the self-adjustment presented by the group would be helpful to them. Do the same after the high-

context group's report by asking the low-context group to respond. For the medium-context group's report, ask both the high- and low-context groups to respond.

Step Eight:
Divide participants into small groups consisting of people all across the high/low-context spectrum. Invite them to write down on a piece of chart paper their responses to:

1. After learning about the different communication styles in this group, what would be some appropriate community principles that would enable this group to be better able to respect and communicate with each other?

2. You may consider modifying and adding to the communication ground rules that we used at the beginning of the session.

Step Nine:
Invite each group to report.

Step Ten:
Debrief with the following questions:

1. What are the similarities among the reports? What are the differences?

2. As a community, can we select out of these reports, ten principles that we can affirm as our community principles that we will affirm as we continue our dialogue in the future?

Step Eleven:
Help the participants to arrive at ten principles. The facilitator creates a document based on the selected principles. The document will be copied, distributed, and read every time the group meets again.

Problems to Anticipate:

1. Some participants may find it difficult to rate themselves. They may say, "It depends on the situation." Invite them to join the medium-context group. If they still feel that it doesn't represent them accurately, they may form their own group. After the sharing of the self-observations, maybe they will decide to join a group.

2. The responses to each report may become too personal and participants may engage in a debate. Be sure to remind people of the communication ground rules and that they are not here to debate who is right and who is wrong but to listen actively with an open mind.

Self-Assessment Work Sheet

On a scale of 1 to 6, 6 being very high-context and 1 being very low-context, where do you think you are? (Circle a number.)

very low-context   1   2   3   4   5   6   very high-context

Describe as many self-observations as you can that support your assessment. Be sure to include as many behavioral observations as possible.

Answer only ONE of the following three questions:

1. If you are on the low-context side of the continuum, what kind of potential problems can you anticipate when communicating with a person from a high-context culture? (List three.) What specific self-adjustment would you make in order to avoid these potential problems? (List three.)

2. If you are on the high-context side of the continuum, what kind of potential problems can you anticipate when communicating with a person from a low-context culture? (List three.) What specific self-adjustment would you make in order to avoid these potential problems? (List three.)

3. If you are in the middle of the continuum, what specific behavior, communication skill, attitude, and value would you emphasize when communicating with a person from a very high-context culture? (List three.) And with a person from a very low-context culture? (List three.)

Appendix D

Techniques for Managing a Bilingual Gathering

1. All written material must be in both languages, especially charts and visual aids.

2. If you are not bilingual yourself, work with a bilingual partner/co-facilitator whenever possible.

3. Find out who the bilingual participants are. They are your resources. You can do this by asking people to put on their name tags what languages they speak.

4. Instead of having one translator, each time a monolingual person speaks, that person is responsible for inviting a bilingual person to interpret for him/her. The bilingual person invited can have the option to pass. This way, the bilingual participants will eventually become part of the team to help everyone understand what is being communicated. In this process, the whole group will learn to value the bilingual participants as their prime resource for communication.

5. Another technique is to divide the participants into language-specific groups. Make sure there is at least one bilingual person in each group. Each group is given a topic to share or discuss. A bilingual person in each group is asked to take notes. When both groups return, a bilingual person in each group will report a summary of what his/her group shared. For example, if you have a Korean-speaking group and an English-speaking group, the bilingual person from the Korean-speaking group will report in English and the bilingual person from the English-speaking group will report in Korean.

6. If a speech or a report is longer than fifteen minutes, the facilitator needs to give people an assignment during the translation so that they can stay focused on the subject while someone is speaking in a language they don't understand. For example, in a Spanish/English meeting, a speaker is giving a speech in Spanish on the subject of "intercultural communication." Before the speech, an English-speaking facilitator can give an assignment to the English-speaking participants such as this one: Spend the next fifteen minutes reflecting on the experiences you have had in the past when you had difficulty communicating in a

multicultural situation. Write down some of these incidents and reflections while our speaker is giving his/her presentation in Spanish. When the speaker finishes, before the translator gives the translation in English, an assignment like this can be given to the Spanish-speaking participants: Spend the next fifteen minutes reflecting on how you can apply what you have just heard to real intercultural situations where you had difficulty communicating. If you wish, you can write down some of these ideas. This technique can also be applied to preaching a sermon in a bilingual service.

Teaching a Congregation to Sing A New Song

Step One:
KNOW YOUR SONG

Before teaching a song, you must know the song very well yourself. Start with a short song.

Step Two:
DIVIDE THE SONG INTO SHORT, LEARNABLE SEGMENTS

Practice singing the song a short phrase at a time. Most songs have natural phrasing in the melody and lyrics. If a phrase is too long (more than seven or eight words), you might want to divide that into two segments. As you practice this, be sure to keep the beat going as you repeat each phrase.

Step Three:
INVITE THE CONGREGATION TO LISTEN FIRST

If people listen well, they will learn the song faster. Sometimes, they may be too eager to sing along with you and may not listen very well. As a result they may learn the wrong melody or discourage others to sing. The best way to do this is to invite the congregation to listen to the whole song first without singing along.

Step Four:
INVITE THE CONGREGATION TO LISTEN AND REPEAT

Then invite the congregation to listen to each segment, without singing along, and then repeat after you. You may need to go over the song twice so that everyone can learn it.

Step Five:
GIVE A BRIEF DESCRIPTION OF THE SONG STRUCTURE

It will help the congregation to better remember the song if you point out any repeated pattern and rhythm in the song. It will also be helpful to point out some unique features in the melody. Keep this very short and then invite the congregation to listen and repeat one more time.

Step Six:
PUTTING THE WHOLE SONG TOGETHER
After the congregation has learned each segment of the song, you can invite them to sing the song, putting all the segments together. Repeat the song a few times.

CONCERNING ACCOMPANIMENT:
This method of teaching does not require any accompaniment. If you use accompaniment, make sure that it does not overpower the singing. The participants have to be able to hear the teacher, themselves, and one another. The accompaniment should follow rather than lead the congregation. Make sure you practice repeating each phrase with the accompaniment. When singing in a round, accompaniment is very useful in keeping the meter.